T3-BPE-324

The Empowered Organization

Redefining the Roles and Practices of Finance

Henry A. Davis

Frederick C. Militello, Jr.

A publication of Financial Executives Research Foundation

Financial Executives Research Foundation
10 Madison Avenue, P.O. Box 1938
Morristown, New Jersey 07962-1938
(201) 898-4608

International Standard Book Number 0-910586-95-0
Library of Congress Catalog Card Number 94-70916
Printed in the United States of America

Second Printing

Financial Executives Research Foundation is the research affiliate of Financial Executives Institute. The basic purpose of the Foundation is to sponsor research and publish informative material in the field of business management, with particular emphasis on the practices of financial management and its evolving role in the management of business.

The views set forth in this publication are those of the author(s) and do not necessarily represent those of the FERF Board as a whole, individual trustees, or the members of the Project Advisory Committee.

FERF publications can be ordered from Professional Book Distributors at (404) 751-1986. Quantity discounts are available.

Project Advisory Committee

James H. Bloem
Vice President & CFO, Herman Miller, Inc.

David C. Carney
Chief Financial Officer
CoreStates Financial Corp

James B. Flaws
Assistant Treasurer, Corning Incorporated

John A. Hevey
Director of Finance/Marketing Operations
Harley-Davidson, Inc.

Richard B. Klein
Senior Vice President & Controller
Corning Incorporated

Dennis McBride
Vice President & Controller, Silicon Graphics, Inc.

Shanti Mehta
Associate
W. L. Gore and Associates, Inc.

Stanley J. Meresman
Senior VP Finance & CFO, Silicon Graphics, Inc.

Alwyn S. Rougier-Chapman
Senior Vice President, Finance, Steelcase Inc.

William M. Sinnett
Senior Research Associate
Financial Executives Research Foundation

Susan Wang (Chairperson)
Senior Vice President & CFO
Solectron Corporation

Jeffrey A. Weber
Chief Executive Officer
The Geo. E. Keith Company

James L. Ziemer
Vice President & CFO
Harley-Davidson, Inc.

Janet F. Hastie
Director of Communications
Financial Executives Research Foundation

Contents

Executive Summary

At the beginning of this decade, dramatic changes affected business and the economy. A severe recession occurred partly in reaction to the leverage of the 1980s and partly as a result of fundamental restructuring by companies to become more competitive in the global market. Quality and putting the customer first were helpful notions, but something was still missing.

A new management paradigm began to emerge. Rather than focusing primarily on external forces such as competition, companies started to look more within themselves to examine their unique capabilities and their principles and values. Most of those principles and values have to do with the way people work together. If a company's first priority is taking care of its people, then motivated and creative people will see to quality and the customer.

In the past several decades, we have evolved from an industrial economy to an information and service economy. Today, even in industrial corporations, most workers are knowledge workers who expect their skills and judgment to be respected and utilized. The old authoritarian ways of managing people in the industrial economy do not work for today's knowledge worker. Multilayered corporate hierarchies are not suited to the fast decision making required in today's ever-changing markets.

Effectiveness is more important than efficiency. To be effective, people closest to the product and the customer need to be empowered. Part of being empowered is having access to the right information. Use of current technology to distribute information is essential. Information protection is no longer a source of power; information sharing is a necessary part of working together as a companywide team. Cross-functional teams are getting the job done more effectively than cumbersome pyramidal bureaucracies. Teams and companies learn together more effectively than individuals can. Organizational learning is the key for a company to find its own distinctive niche and competitive advantage.

The finance function is playing an integral role in the management revolution. Financial executives find that control and empowerment can be reconciled. Empowered, self-managed teams are working within the finance function. Finance people are members of cross-functional teams. Finance people can be more effective by getting to know the business and helping their manufacturing and marketing colleagues make better decisions, instead of being functional stars concerned with purely financial matters.

Principal Research Findings

- Finance people are well integrated into the process of cultural change.
- Finance people have sometimes suffered under the image of "naysayers" and "bean-counters" who were primarily concerned with control and budget variances. A new model for financial behavior is emerging based on trust, teamwork, integration, and contribution.
- Interpersonal, influencing, and other "soft" skills have become as important as technical skills for financial executives to succeed in their careers.
- Financial executives have embraced principles and values in defining their standards of behavior and the role of the finance function in the organization.
- The emphasis of financial practice is shifting away from control and more toward business advocacy and providing value-added services.
- While integrity of the numbers and the corporate audit process remain a priority, financial people are generally comfortable with both employee empowerment and softer controls. Control can be reconciled with empowerment as long as people understand why controls are needed, and they understand that controls are not a reflection on their own personal integrity or capabilities. Teams can help in the control process because more people are aware of the controls that are necessary.
- Empowerment must have boundaries, and with empowerment comes greater responsibility and accountability. Empowerment may also cause intermittent stress and frustration as people

take on more decision-making responsibility and negotiate with peers in a less structured environment.

- Finance people are key participants in teams throughout the company such as business unit management teams, reengineering teams, problem solving teams, and continuous improvement teams. They transcend their functional identities as they work with people from other functions to solve multifaceted business problems.
- Sharing information both internally and externally and developing systems to empower people with the information they need is recognized as a competitive requirement in today's global market.
- As finance people become more line-integrated, fewer report to headquarters and more report to line units. Some finance functions, however, are often still centralized for efficiency and economies of scale.
- To be effective, cultural change should start from the top of the organization. When it does, the finance function plays an important catalytic role in implementing the organization's principles and values because of the many ways it interacts with every other function. An exception may be found with companies in financial difficulty, where the finance function often plays a predominant role and may act as the initiator of cultural change.

Research Objectives

The premise of this research project is that the finance function within the corporation plays an integral role in new management thinking and is directly affected by new management concepts such as management by principles and values, empowerment, information sharing, organizational learning, and internal and external partnerships. A great deal has been written about how this new management thinking affects companies in general, but virtually nothing has been written about how it affects the finance function. This project was commissioned to address that information gap and, more specifically, how the new management paradigm has affected financial practices, the behavior of financial executives, and corporate expectations about the role of the finance function.

The Empowered Organization: Redefining the Roles and Practices of Finance is the fourth in the FERF initiative on Organization and Strategy in Financial Management. There are a number of overlapping themes within this series. For example, finance functions in the companies studied here generally conform to the competitive-team orientation described in *Changing Roles in Financial Management*; finance people in these companies act more as business advocates than as corporate policemen. For a number of companies represented in this book, implementing principles and values is closely related to the type of quality program studied in *Finance in the Quality Revolution.*

Selection of Case Study Companies

Companies were chosen for this project for two primary reasons:

1. They have all demonstrated a commitment to cultural change. For example, they may have adopted the Malcolm Balridge Quality Award criteria for evaluating their internal organizational relationships and productive processes. Moreover, their chief executive officers (CEOs) tend to stand out as leaders of organizational change, and the companies are often cited for their progressive management thinking in publications such as the *Harvard Business Review* or *Fortune.* The researchers looked for companies that expressed and demonstrated a commitment to cultural change in the context of all their stakeholders, not just the bottom line.

2. Finance has played an important role in the process of organizational change. Rather than seeing finance in the role of a corporate naysayer or policeman, financial executives in these companies are business advocates. They are adding value, integrating themselves, and helping to improve every aspect of corporate life, from production processes to hiring practices.

The researchers selected potential case-study companies based on published information. Then they called senior financial officers, mostly Financial Executives Institute members, to describe the project and to ensure that the finance function was an integral part of the cultural change process. Nine companies agreed to participate.

Research Methodology

The researchers interviewed between one and five financial officers in each case-study company. Chief financial officers (CFOs) were interviewed in every company. CEOs were interviewed in three. Interviews were taped, allowing the researchers to capture details and nuances that would not have been possible otherwise. As a result, the book relies to a very minimal degree on secondary published material concerning the case-study companies. Several companies provided useful exhibits covering topics such as behaviors valued in the finance function, guidelines for teams, and organization charts.

How to Use This Book

This executive summary is followed by Chapter 1, A New Management Paradigm, which compares traditional and emerging ways of management thinking, raises questions about how the new management thinking applies to the finance function, and summarizes principal findings and common themes across all the case-study companies.

Chapter 2 explains a five-layer model in which the researchers' principal observations are categorized as principles, values, behavioral objectives, implementation methods, and behavioral results.

Chapters 3 through 12 contain detailed case studies of the nine companies interviewed.

The final section is a descriptive bibliography of books and articles the researchers consider most useful for the financial executive who wishes to pursue these issues in greater detail.

1

A New Management Paradigm

A central finding of this study is that a new way of management thinking has emerged with common elements shared by many companies. No one concept captures the new thinking, but a flavor is provided by the following contrasts:

- Rather than just managing by objectives, also manage by values.
- What gets done and what is measured is not all that counts; how one achieves it can make the difference.
- Horizontal organizational structures are replacing vertical ones.
- Rather than managing by control, try empowering people.
- Integrated teams and processes are more important than isolated functions (such as finance, manufacturing or marketing.)
- Don't reorganize for success; look to cultural change.
- Doing more with less is a new reality of corporate life.

This behavioral revolution is taking shape in some of the world's leading corporations. For example, GE's chairman, John F. Welch, talks about the Lilliputian virtues of "speed, simplicity and self confidence." He goes on to speak about "teams [that] will move together from left to right, from product idea to product delivery, reaching into the core as they need to get the job done" and of managers who "will be people who are comfortable facilitating, greasing, finding ways to make it all seamless...."

Or at Levi Strauss & Co. we hear CEO Robert D. Haas saying, "What we've learned is that the soft stuff and the hard stuff are increasingly becoming intertwined. A company's values—what it stands for, what its people believe in—are crucial to its competitive success. Indeed, values drive the business."

The revolution has not been ignored or dismissed by the academic community. For example, Peter M. Senge of Massachusetts Institute of Technology (MIT), in *The Fifth Discipline,* writes about the learning organization, "an organization that is continuously expanding its capacity to create its future." Charles Handy, in the *Age of Unreason,* writes about a future organization whose "language is not that of engineering but of politics, with talk of cultures, and networks, of teams and coalitions, of influence or power rather than control, of leadership not just management." And William C. Byham in the *Lightening of Empowerment* notes: "More and more in the years to come, the successful organizations will be the ones best able to apply the creative energy of individuals toward constant improvement.... The only way to get people to adopt constant improvement as a way of life in doing daily business is by empowering them."

A few examples of the old and the new emphasis in management thinking are shown in figure 1.

FIGURE 1: Examples of Traditional and Emerging Management Thinking

The new management thinking does not replace traditional management thinking, but adds to it and changes the emphasis somewhat. For example, management by values and effectiveness are important concepts, but management by objectives and efficiency still have their place.

Current Emphasis	*Emerging Emphasis*
Manage by objectives	Manage by values
Mission statement	Values or essence statement
Efficiency	Effectiveness
Look externally	Look externally *and* internally
Customer first	Customer *and* people first
Power = information control	Power = information sharing
Supervise employees	Empower employees
Individual learning	Team and organizational learning
Measure results	Understand process
Controlling role of finance	Influencing role of finance
Financial measures (such as income)	Nonfinancial measures (such as timeliness)
Mergers and acquisitions	Partnerships and alliances

Additional flavor for the new management thinking can be gained from a few selected quotations from academic and business leaders in figure 2.

FIGURE 2: Quotes from Academic and Business Leaders

Robert D. Haas, chairman and CEO, Levi Strauss & Co.

We always talked about the hard stuff and the soft stuff. The soft stuff was the company's commitment to the work force. And the hard stuff was what really mattered, getting product out the door.

What we've learned is that the soft stuff and the hard stuff are increasingly intertwined. A company's values—what it stands for, what its people believe in—are crucial to its competitive success. Indeed values drive the business.

At LS&CO., we talk about creating an empowered organization. By that we mean a company where the people who are the closest to the product and the customer take the initiative without having to check with anyone.

Richard Teerlink, president and CEO (former CFO), Harley-Davidson, Inc.

We strive to eliminate many of the complications and bureaucratic roadblocks most firms face and concentrate on the basics of our business. To do this, we live by a set of simple values: Tell the truth. Keep your promises. Be fair. Respect the individual. Encourage individual curiosity. Our markets, products and manufacturing processes can and do change. Our values, however, remain constant and are vital to delivering increased stakeholder satisfaction.

Alvin Toffler, author of *Future Shock*

The safer and surer a business information system, and the better it is protected, pre-defined, pre-structured and policed, the more it will constrain creativity and constipate the organization.

Power, in the business of tomorrow, will flow to those who have the best information about the limits of information.

Ray Stats, chairman and president, Analog Devices, Inc.

We have found that the best way to introduce knowledge and modify behavior is by working with small teams that have the power and resources to enact change.

I would argue that the rate at which individuals and organizations learn may become the only sustainable comparative advantage.

John F. Welch, CEO, General Electric

Tomorrow's organization will be boundaryless. It will work with outsiders as closely as if they were insiders. The lines between the company and its vendors and customers must be blurred into a smooth, fluid process with no other objective than satisfying the customer and winning the marketplace.

Neatness and orderliness is not what we are after. We are after getting information to the people who can act on it.

Peter M. Senge, MIT, author of *The Fifth Discipline*

Most of us at one time or another have been part of a great team, a group of people who functioned together in an extraordinary way—who trusted one another, who complemented each other's strengths and compensated for each others' limitations, who produced extraordinary results. I have met many people who have experienced this sort of profound teamwork—in sports, or in the performing arts, or in business. Many say that they have spent much of their life looking for that experience again. What they experienced was a learning organization. The team that became great didn't start off great—it learned how to produce extraordinary results.

Tenets of the New Management Thinking

Several concepts that are central to the new management thinking have been adopted to some degree by all of the companies in the study:

Managing by principles and values. Defining and getting people to buy into a set of core principles and values is a deeper motivational force and is more effective in bringing out the best in people than just defining objectives. It involves defining and getting people to agree on what the company is all about, how the company can succeed, the proper role and mission of employees, and the nature of the social contract between the company and its employees—or partners.

Leadership. If values are an important motivating, unifying, and focusing force, then something more inspirational than just management is required. Leadership must be firmly grounded in principles. Though the tone is set at the top, leadership works at all levels and in all directions—upward, downward, and horizontally.

Empowerment. The company can perform more successfully and more quickly, and people can be better motivated, if both authority and responsibility are delegated. People most qualified and closest to the action—for example, people on the plant floor or people dealing with customers—should be allowed to make decisions.

Teamwork. Teams are taking the place of hierarchy as the most effective way to get things done. A team may be temporary or permanent, and it may be organized within a function or across functions. Within a team, there is strong emphasis on what each person contributes and how each person interacts with the other team members, and littleemphasis on the person's title in the company. Members of a function such as finance bring particular knowledge and skills to a team, but participate in team decision making in a way that transcends their functional identities.

Partnering. Companies are partnering with customers, suppliers, competitors, and their own people. Externally, it is recognized that no company succeeds by doing everything itself and that cooperative relationships between a company and its suppliers and dealers are more productive than confrontational relationships. Internally, partnering is consistent with empowerment and treating people as the company's most important resource.

Information sharing. Guarding and not sharing information was a way to increase power in a hierarchical, individual-focused organization. Today, dissemination of the right information to the people who need it when they need it is both power and a requirement for success in almost every industry. It requires companies to invest in the most advanced information systems, and it requires people throughout the organization to share information with their partners.

Organizational learning. People in all functions of the company can be more effective if they know more about the business. Teams and the company overall acquire greater and more useful knowledge by learning together than individuals can by learning independently. Team learning is one of the processes by which a company develops its distinctive competence.

Implications for the Financial Executive

The new management thinking raises interesting questions for financial executives, which are the foundation for this research project:

- □ How will the finance function operate in a more process- or team-oriented organization?
- □ Is a "functional" approach to organizing finance still relevant?
- □ How will the new managerial concepts, such as empowerment and organizational learning, apply to the discipline and practice of financial management?
- □ What new skills will financial executives need to learn?
- □ How will financial objectives change?

- ☐ Will bottom-line results matter as much as how they are achieved?
- ☐ How will corporate values affect financial controls and guidelines?
- ☐ How might external relationships, for instance with banks or underwriting groups, be affected?
- ☐ What challenges face the financial executive communicating values-oriented goals to the investment community?

2

A Model for Implementing Principles and Values

After interviewing the nine case study companies, the researchers developed a conceptual model of organizational change. The model is illustrated in figure 3 and described in figure 4. In essence, for all companies interviewed, the researchers found a rather common set of core principles, management practices, and desired end results consistent with the goal of effective cultural change. Moreover, these behavioral changes at the organizational level were accompanied by a rather consistent set of expectations concerning the behaviors and practices of financial executives.

The cases not only demonstrate a model for organizational change but illustrate how financial executives and their practices are taking an active part in both responding to and reshaping that process.

Most of the researchers' observations can be organized into the following five categories:

1. Principles—basic standards of behavior that should be universally accepted and followed by all people and all organizations.
2. Values—qualities or standards considered worthwhile by a particular organization or individual.
3. Behavioral objectives—specific types of behavior that management encourages to implement principles and organizational values.
4. Implementation methods—specific programs to implement principles and values.

5. Behavioral results—new behavioral norms in the organization caused by the adoption of its principles and values.

The five levels of this model are illustrated as a series of concentric circles in figure 3. Principles at the center are analogous to a stone thrown in a pond, starting a series of outward ripples. Figure 4 provides examples of principles and values; figure 5 illustrates how the model applies to case study companies.

FIGURE 3: Model for Implementing Principles and Values

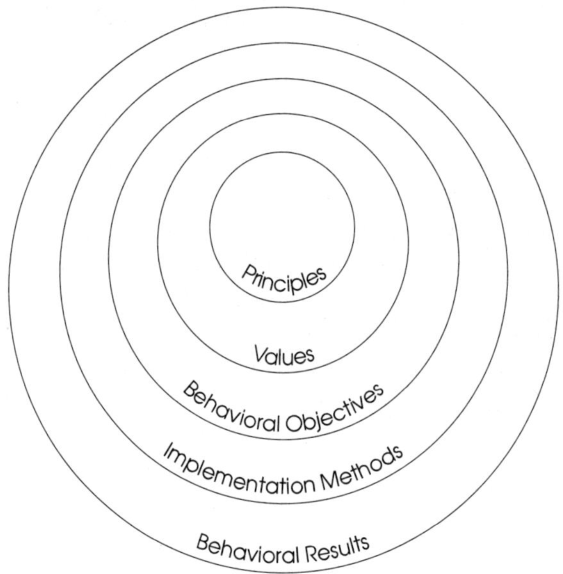

FIGURE 4: Examples of Principles and Values

Principles

- Truthfulness
- Fairness
- Integrity
- Trust
- Recognition
- Accountability
- Respect for others
- Personal growth and redemption

Values

- Performance
- Quality
- Diversity
- Intellectual curiosity
- Entrepreneurial spirit
- No single right answer
- Social/environmental responsibility
- Concern for all stakeholders
- Pride in product, technology, or design

Behavioral Objectives

- Participative management
- Flattened organization
- Partnering, internal and external
- Organizational learning
- Teamwork
- Information sharing
- Empowerment
- Mentoring

Implementation Methods

- Suboptimizing short-term financial objectives
- Employee stock ownership and profit sharing
- Total quality management (TQM) programs
- Peer interviewing and performance evaluation
- Joint ventures and strategic alliances
- Finance people in cross-functional teams
- Finance people assigned to business units
- Efforts to recruit more women and minorities
- Celebrating success and work well done

Behavioral Results

- Finance people with soft skills
- Finance people with knowledge of the business
- Finance people with general management orientation
- Finance people serving internal customers
- Finance people as consultants and advocates
- Finance people as facilitators more than enforcers
- Finance people as cultural change agents
- Greater willingness to ask questions and help with answers
- Greater willingness to take risks
- Fewer decisions based on rank
- Women and minorities in senior finance positions
- Requirement to deal with ambiguity and stress
- Occasional resistance to cultural change

For example, the core principles of fairness, trust, and truthfulness are essential for achieving behavioral objectives such as organizational learning, teamwork, or information sharing. In turn, those desired behaviors are essential for continually improving an organization's product quality and customer service and its people's knowledge of the business. Consistent with these desired behaviors, the researchers found financial people working with business people to solve business problems in a broad range of disciplines such as design, production, sourcing, costing, pricing, inventory management, distribution, logistics, and warranties. Finance people are participating with other functions in the capital budgeting process as nonquantitative considerations become equally, if not more, important than net present value analyses. The finance function is sharing financial information selectively with bankers, suppliers, and retailers. It is looking to the financial well-being of suppliers and retailers in the company's interest and with the philosophy that both sides of a healthy partnership should find it profitable. The researchers found financial executives embracing corporate diversity objectives, frequently taking the lead and setting the example for others to follow.

The distinction between principles and values is particularly important in the context of this study, though it is recognized that companies and scholars use these terms in various ways. Stephen Covey, author of *The Seven Habits of Highly Effective People* and *Principle Centered Leadership,* describes principles as self-evident, self-validating natural laws that do not change or shift. They apply at all times in all places. They have been tested and proven effective through centuries of civilization. Values, on the other hand, reflect an organization's or an individual's background. They are shaped by cultural influences, personal discoveries, and organizational experience. A criminal organization can share values, but it does not follow the principles described here.

According to Covey, principles are objective and external, whereas values are subjective and internal. Principles are like compasses that always point the way. They provide a constant "true north" that keeps us from getting confused by conflicting notions. Values are more like maps; they are subjective attempts to describe the territory.

FIGURE 5: The Model Applied to the Case Study Companies

CoreStates Financial Corp

Principles
- People
- Financial strength
- Risk management
- Technology

Values
- People
- Integrity
- Performance
- Teamwork
- Communication
- Diversity

Behavioral Objectives
- Leveling the playing field
- Dismantling silos
- Finance and human resource functions as catalysts for change
- Partnerships with other financial institutions
- CoreValues providing a platform for quality program

Implementation Methods
- Diversity initiative
- Companywide surveys of employees concerning culture and work environment
- Hiring and performance appraisal criteria consistent with CoreValues
- Total quality management program focused on internal customers
- Financial liaison people in business units
- Merger, due diligence, and integration task forces
- Process improvement teams
- Outsourcing and insourcing
- Exploring joint acquisition with another bank

Behavioral Results
- Finance function involved while decisions are being made
- Finance function balancing service and control roles
- Still learning what empowerment means
- Still integrating CoreValues with day-to-day business decisions
- Considering cultural fit with acquisition targets
- Loosening expense controls
- Securities analysts not accustomed to focusing on soft issues such as values and quality

FIGURE 5: The Model Applied to the Case Study Companies (continued)

Corning

Principles
- Integrity
- Valuing the individual

Values
- Quality
- Performance
- Leadership
- Technology
- Independence

Behavioral Objectives
- Empowerment and teamwork
- Finance people with interpersonal skills and general management orientation
- Everyone influencing and identifying with key results indicators

Implementation Methods
- Cross-training and soft skills training for teams
- Performance appraisal matrix
- Finance teams in business units
- Self-managed teams in Administrative Center
- Hiring finance people with soft skills
- Community amenities for minorities
- Joint ventures

Behavioral Results
- Finance people as integral parts of business teams
- Finance people becoming business managers
- Finance people's jobs becoming more team- and strategy-oriented at higher levels
- Close working relationship among finance people in joint ventures
- Substantial number of women in senior finance positions
- Supervisors and managers becoming coaches and leaders
- Eliminating layers of management
- Spending authority pushed down
- Improved communication and trust
- Stress as team members take on more responsibility, learn to make decisions
- Errors and cycle time reduced in closing through improved information sharing among teams

FIGURE 5: The Model Applied to the Case Study Companies (continued)

W. L. Gore and Associates, Inc.

Principles [Bill Gore's Principles, summarized below, are reproduced in full in Chapter 6.]

- Being fair
- Allowing, helping, and encouraging associates to grow; giving them freedom
- Making commitments and keeping them
- Consulting with associates before taking actions that will put the company "below the waterline"

Values

- Make money and have fun
- Concentrate on cash flow, not profits
- No leverage
- Preserving atmosphere of young entrepreneurial company

Behavioral Objectives

- No person reporting to any other person
- Person's strengths used to the maximum; weaknesses minimized
- Individuals paid based on contribution
- Unleash creativity
- Eliminate nonvalue-added activities

Implementation Methods

- Lattice organizational structure
- Peer evaluation and ranking
- Compensation committees; pay based on contribution
- Product champion and review committee for capital budgeting
- Informal, consultative role of CFO
- Access to other business units' financials for benchmarking
- Every associate having a sponsor; most associates being sponsors
- Team of associates interviewing prospective hires
- Monthly financial bulletin to all associates

Behavioral Results

- Freedom to explore new ideas
- Requirement to make individual contribution visible
- Requirement for individual initiative to join team and to move to new opportunities
- No social visits with bankers
- Dealing with ambiguity in unstructured environment
- Lean finance staff; one-person treasury function
- Control easily reconciled with empowerment
- Voluntary departure for people who are used to more structure

FIGURE 5: The Model Applied to the Case Study Companies (continued)

Harley-Davidson, Inc.

Management Values
- Telling the truth
- Being fair
- Respecting the individual
- Keeping your promises
- Encourage intellectual curiosity

Organizational Issues
- Quality
- Participation
- Flexibility
- Productivity
- Cash flow
- Balancing interests of all stakeholders
- Willingness to suboptimize
- Customer satisfaction regardless of short-term profits
- Selling lifestyle

Behavioral Objectives
- Information flow
- Control through accountability
- Empowerment with fences
- Vision: continuous improvement and the elimination of non-value-added activities
- Finance a service organization

Implementation Methods
- Flattened organization of three intersecting circles: marketing, manufacturing, and support
- Finance people decentralized to each of the three circles
- Individual and group fence setting
- Softer controls: less use of policy manual, less review of travel expenses
- Empowerment and leadership training
- Videoconferencing
- Partnerships with dealers
- Harley Owners Group (HOG)

Behavioral Results
- General management orientation of finance professionals
- Finance people working with business people from the beginning of the planning process
- Finance people focusing on process ***and*** results
- Finance people serving internal customers
- Finance people helping business people understand value-added activities
- Telling people information when you know it

FIGURE 5: The Model Applied to the Case Study Companies (continued)

Geo. E. Keith Company

Principles
- Being honest and fair with people
- No one person or group is better than any other
- Politics have no place
- Sense of belonging
- Role clarification

Values
- Pride in product and company history

Behavioral Objectives
- Teamwork to survive
- Information sharing with employees, investors, vendors, and bankers
- Job enlargement

Implementation Methods
- Weekly flash report of performance and financial information
- Collaboration between control and production for product costing
- People doing more than one job
- Self-managed team in finance function

Behavioral Results
- Bonding created by adversity
- Personal sacrifices required for company survival
- CFO as cultural change agent
- Managing upward
- Willingness to take risks
- Finance people with broad knowledge of the business

FIGURE 5: The Model Applied to the Case Study Companies (continued)

Herman Miller, Inc.

Management Principles
- Equity
- Integrity
- Accountability
- Dignity and potential of every person

Organizational Values
- Excellence; good design
- Ownership
- Participation and teamwork
- Diversity fundamental to success
- Learning and new ideas
- New products and customer satisfaction
- Financial results are results, not ends
- Effectiveness more important than efficiency
- All work can be rewarding and enjoyable

Behavioral Objectives
- Participative management
- Covenantal relationships are more important than structure
- Open communication

Implementation Methods
- Decentralized, matrix-managed finance function
- Career ladder: rotation through the business
- Everyone is a mentor and has a mentor
- Group decision making: participation, discussion, then action
- Cross-functional teams
- CFO, controller, and chief legal officer a team
- Facilitator role of finance function
- Scanlon plan linking compensation to performance objectives
- Employee stock ownership
- Rating your work team leader in performance reviews

Behavioral Results
- Finance people using interpersonal, influencing, and organizational skills
- General management orientation of finance people
- One-third of finance professionals assigned to subsidiaries and other nonfinance functions, e.g., marketing, logistics
- Finance people in senior management positions
- Balancing financial and business decision-making skills
- Nonfinancial issues considered in capital budgeting
- Willingness to ask and tell
- Dealing with ambiguity
- Hiring to fill specific positions; little hiring at entry level
- More time required for participative decision making

FIGURE 5: The Model Applied to the Case Study Companies (continued)

Levi Strauss & Co.

Management Principles
- Commitment to the success of others
- Personal accountability
- Trust
- Ethical management practices

Organizational Values
- Diversity
- Recognition
- Directness
- Openness to influence
- Willingness to acknowledge our own contribution to problems

Behavioral Objectives
- Teamwork
- Empowerment
- Communication
- Employee partnerships
- Business partnerships

Implementation Methods
- Eliminating unnecessary controls
- Leadership training programs
- Maintaining fewer, closer supplier relationships
- Holding contractors to environmental standards
- Electronic data interchange with suppliers and retailers
- Sharing information with banks and other business partners
- Not shopping around proprietary financial products
- Pay for Performance Plan linked to shareholder value
- Spherical performance evaluation
- Informal dress code

Results
- Finance function more team-oriented, less expert-oriented
- Finance people learning the business
- Finance people assigned to brands
- Finance people in cross-functional, problem-solving teams
- Finance people in teams to support largest customers
- Finance people moving to and from marketing and manufacturing assignments
- Auditors playing more supportive role
- Fewer layers of management and less review
- Spirit of teamwork affecting the way people feel and work
- People emerging from silos to become effective team contributors
- Slowing down decision making for consensus
- Reputation for values attracting top business school graduates

FIGURE 5: The Model Applied to the Case Study Companies (continued)

Silicon Graphics, Inc.

Principles

- Doing what is right
- Acting with integrity
- Being open and honest
- Respecting people
- Accountability

Values

- No single right answer; many ways to do things
- Diversity of people and ideas
- Not a political company
- Maintaining entrepreneurial spirit
- Everybody a worker
- Encouraging risk taking; OK to fail now and then, but learn from it

Objectives

- Being hands on
- Being a leader
- Going for it
- Initiating
- Empowering people while company grows 35 percent per year
- Cooperating, not competing within the company; everyone focused on enhancing the value of the company
- Treating key customers as technology drivers
- Treating vendors as partners
- Communicating and listening
- Being open to feedback and seeking it out
- Developing influencing skills

Methods

- Combination of centralized and decentralized finance function with decentralized parts matrix managed
- Doing inside what is strategic to the business; contracting out what is not strategic
- Worldwide controllers conference
- Award trip for people who exemplify company values to meet with management
- Up to 10 people interview professional candidates

Results

- Organized chaos with clear vision and direction
- Rapid, open communications; use of voice mail; giving "heads up"
- Speaking up if you see something wrong, even outside your area
- No need to explain why you are asking for information
- Little crossover between finance and operations in high-technology company

FIGURE 5: The Model Applied to the Case Study Companies (continued)

Steelcase Inc.

Principles

- Treating ourselves and each other with respect
- Acting with integrity in everything we do

Values

- Satisfying customers completely
- Valuing and building workforce diversity
- Working as partners with customers, fellow employees, design professionals, dealers, suppliers, and shareholders
- Supporting the company's communities
- Respecting the environment

Objectives

- World-class performance
- Organization that is flexible and fast on its feet
- Empowering employees to act on their own, take responsibility for quality
- Reaching potential and having fun doing so
- Producing information, not data; making sure it is timely and accessible
- Selling complete environment for knowledge worker
- Modeling internally what the company sells

Methods

- Team-based organization in the factory
- Reengineering teams
- Continuous improvement teams
- Team sponsors
- Team training
- Holding teams accountable
- Focusing team efforts on problems they can solve
- Disbanding teams when their missions are accomplished
- Increased sharing of financial information

Results

- Almost everyone in the company a member of at least one team
- Teams benefitting from members strengths and weaknesses
- Increase in team members' self-confidence and knowledge of the business
- Reinforcement of historically low employee turnover
- Increased controls resulting from empowerment and teamwork
- Increased financial literacy throughout the company
- Breaking down "silos" through sharing financial information
- Few processes "owned" by finance function

3

Summary of Principal Findings and Common Themes

Principles and Values

Each company in the study has well-defined and articulated principles and values that guide managers and employees at every level in how they run the company, do their jobs, and deal with one another. Robert Haas, CEO of Levi Strauss & Co., states that values drive the company. Terry Larsen, CEO of CoreStates Financial, commissioned a people task force that drew up the company's CoreValues after seeing a need for cultural change. He had perceived a culture that was uneven from one part of the organization to another and a number of people who didn't enjoy coming to work in the morning. He believes that instilling those values in the organization is a prerequisite for implementing the corporation's total quality management program. The CoreValues and quality are the foundation of the corporation's strategy to achieve a competitive advantage. Alwyn Rougier-Chapman, senior vice president–finance at Steelcase, agrees with the importance of management by values, but believes that management by objectives is still important.

Officers throughout the finance function are thoroughly familiar with their companies' principles and values. They are willing to try to pick out the values that have the most meaning for them, though they admit this is difficult. George James, CFO of Levi Strauss & Co., believes that "ethical management practices" is a value that particularly stands out above the others. Jim Flaws, assistant treasurer of Corning, points to a sign posted in offices throughout the company that says, "Integrity is the bottom line."

The companies in the study have a number of management principles in common. Harley-Davidson and Steelcase talk of balancing the interests of all stakeholders. Herman Miller and Corning mention concern for the individual. CoreStates, Corning, and Levi Strauss & Co. have particularly visible commitments to diversity. At Silicon Graphics and the Geo. E. Keith Company, politics have no place, and at Silicon Graphics and Herman Miller, using position power and making decisions based on rank is against the company culture. The reaction to such behavior at Silicon Graphics is, "We don't do that here."

There are common organizational values running through the companies as well. For Harley-Davidson with its motorcycles, Levi Strauss & Co. with its jeans and Dockers® casual apparel, and Geo. E. Keith with its traditional New England–made shoes, there is a mystique about the product that is felt throughout the company and is also used as a strong marketing tool. At Herman Miller, which produces the Eames chair displayed at the Museum of Modern Art, and at Steelcase, which is devoted to the knowledge worker's total environment, there are strong shared interests in good design that are evident not just in the products, but also in the companies' buildings—particularly the ones where the designers themselves work. At Levi Strauss & Co. and Corning, having products people can identify with is closely related to being on *Fortune's* list of most admired corporations.

At Herman Miller, financial results are results, not ends. At Silicon Graphics, getting the result is essential, but how you went about getting it is also important. Harley-Davidson and Levi Strauss & Co. talk of suboptimizing current financial results in the company's long-term interests. At Harley-Davidson, this means balancing stakeholders' interests—compromising profitability just a little so as to avoid hurting one thousand families, or, more painful, laying off 40 percent of the workforce so that the other 60 percent and the company can survive.

At Silicon Graphics and W. L. Gore, both relatively young companies, maintaining the original entrepreneurial spirit is an important value. Herman Miller has grown substantially in the past 25 years and talks about maintaining the small-company spirit. Consistent with such a spirit, people are encouraged to take risks at Levi Strauss & Co., Silicon Graphics, W. L. Gore, and Herman Miller. In those companies, it's OK to fail once in a while if you learn something in the process. But when something goes wrong at Silicon Graphics, it's important to give a "heads up" right away, and even for sensitive matters it's better to convey the message right away through voice mail than to wait. Similarly, at W. L. Gore, not every new product development project goes as planned, but when the outlook turns sour, it is important to acknowledge that and cut the company's losses.

Quality

Quality is one of Corning's values as well, but here too, quality is a subset of values and cultural change, not the other way around. At Harley-Davidson, quality is one of CEO Richard Teerlink's Business Issues, along with participation, flexibility, productivity and cash flow. Teerlink does not subscribe to total quality management (TQM) per se because he believes such programs often amount to form over substance. Part of the quality program at CoreStates, Corning, and Harley-Davidson is serving the internal customer. Harley-Davidson's Teerlink believes that this is particularly important for finance people to remember as they think about where they can add value.

Behavioral Objectives

In all of the companies interviewed, empowering people, flattening the organization, creating teams, sharing information, and developing both internal and external partnerships are considered important behavioral objectives for implementing stated principles and values. David Carney, CFO of CoreStates Financial, and Rougier-Chapman of Steelcase, talk of dismantling silos. Carney stresses the need to level the playing field to make the value of diversity a reality. At Herman Miller, the process of participative management and group decision making is just as important as what decisions are reached and what financial results are achieved. Silicon Graphics values taking initiative and taking risks, but giving a "heads up" right away when mistakes are made. W. L. Gore and Associates believes in recognizing and utilizing a person's strengths and overlooking the person's weaknesses, particularly if those weaknesses are not relevant to the way the person is most capable of making a contribution.

Empowerment

Both CoreStates and Steelcase admit that they are still learning what empowerment means. Richard Teerlink, CEO of Harley-Davidson, believes that empowerment needs fences to be effective. The benefits of empowerment could be mitigated if individuals routinely try to do too much, i.e., go beyond their fences. Joe Maurer, treasurer of Levi Strauss & Co., believes that some financial processes such as negotiating with lenders and managing foreign exchange exposure do not lend themselves to empowerment. The treasury and cash management functions are mostly centralized in the case-study companies, but the treasury function itself is often considered an empowered team. At Silicon Graphics, managers feel that they own what they are doing and are charged with making it happen.

Empowerment and Control

Virtually all the companies interviewed agree that empowerment can be reconciled with control. Everyone must understand why a company needs controls. They must understand that controls are not a reflection on them as capable and empowered people. Corning, CoreStates, and Levi Strauss & Co. are relying more on soft controls starting with their organizations' stated principles and values. Bill Williams, controller of Steelcase, believes that a team organization can actually increase controls because more people are aware of just what controls need to be in place. Steelcase is trying to build control and quality into each person's day-to-day job. Levi Strauss & Co. has made the internal audit function a more supportive, consultative process. The auditor is there to help the business manager, and only substantial problems are reported to senior management. At Silicon Graphics, the more you are empowered, the more you are expected to act responsibly, which includes providing an environment of control.

Teams

Teams, both cross-functional and within functions, are an important part of the organization in all of the case-study companies. At Corning, Harley-Davidson, and Steelcase, empowered teams were used first in the plants and later applied to white-collar areas such as finance. Teamwork between finance and operations helps solve a variety of problems such as standard costing at Geo. E. Keith, problems with unauthorized distribution arbitraging of Levi 501® jeans across borders at Levi Strauss & Co., and accounting for the cost of repairs under warranty at Herman Miller. Cross-functional reengineering and continuous improvement team efforts are underway at Corning, CoreStates Financial, and Steelcase.

Steelcase recognizes and benefits from team members' compensating strengths and weaknesses. But Controller Bill Williams worries that pushing the team concept too far could discourage individual initiative and drive. W. L. Gore tries to overlook weaknesses altogether if they don't adversely affect the associate's strengths and ability to make a contribution.

At both Corning and Harley-Davidson, the biggest problem cited by members of self-managed teams is stress. For most problems, they used to turn to their managers. Now they must negotiate the solutions to those problems among themselves.

Information Sharing

Providing people at all levels of the organization with the information they need is an essential part of empowerment. At Levi Strauss & Co. and Silicon Graphics, people assume you need information if you ask for it. At Harley-Davidson, having a finance person working in the marketing "circle" avoids communication problems between marketing and finance. Before, marketing could embark on an expensive new sales program and finance might not find out about it until six months later. At Geo. E. Keith, information sharing is essential for management to maintain credibility within the company and with investors, lenders, suppliers, and retailers.

Information sharing in today's competitive environment requires having the right, up-to-date information ready to distribute to the people who need it. Large companies such as Levi Strauss & Co. and smaller companies such as Geo. E. Keith admit that they need to continue to develop their information systems and centralized databases.

Role of Management

Empowerment and team structures require managers to change the way they do things and change their ways of thinking. Some of them find that difficult. When Robert Haas, CEO, started to flatten the organization at Levi Strauss & Co., he recognized that markets were moving too fast for managers to supervise employees and make every decision. Now managers at Levi Strauss & Co. set parameters. Managers are learning to be coaches as Harley-Davidson gains experience with teams and its flattened organization of three intersecting circles—manufacturing, marketing, and support. At Steelcase, managers who are not team members are encouraged to play no role other than providing advice if asked or perhaps acting as sponsors. Sponsors oversee teams and make sure they meet their goals, but do not supervise day to day.

Leadership

Aligning an organization with principles and values requires not just management but leadership. Max DePree, former CEO of Herman Miller, wrote two books on leadership, *Leadership is an Art* and *Leadership Jazz.* Three of DePree's leadership principles were cited by Richard Teerlink, CEO of Harley-Davidson: Define reality. Be a steward. Say thank-you. At Silicon Graphics, extensive leadership training is provided to senior managers. The company's executives must be good leaders as well as excellent managers.

Learning Organization

Participation in teams and training programs helps people in companies learn more about other functions and how their own responsibilities fit into the goals of the organization. CoreStates and Corning have both defined the amount of time every employee should spend in training each year.

Internal Partnerships

The personal lives and feelings of employees are high on the list of concerns for the CEOs and CFOs of the case-study companies. Two of the companies, Levi Strauss & Co. and Steelcase, are recent winners of *Personnel Journal* Optimas awards. The corporate name W. L. Gore and Associates underscores that everyone in the company is called an associate. At Levi Strauss & Co., benefits such as day care centers, family leave policies, and flextime are believed to reduce stress and help employees concentrate on their jobs.

Van Campbell, vice chairman of finance and administration at Corning, has seen finance professionals become more concerned with balance over the last generation. In contrast to the whiz kids of the McNamara era, people today want to do well but lead well-rounded lives. It is more difficult today with competing pressures such as shared family responsibilities in dual-income households.

Harley-Davidson and Levi Strauss & Co. had to go through the pain of major downsizing and layoff programs while reinventing themselves and developing new corporate cultures. Harley-Davidson had to lay off 40 percent to save the company and the jobs of the remaining 60 percent—a poignant case of balancing stakeholders' interests. Even in articulating the Aspirations Statement, Levi Strauss & Co. CEO Robert Haas admitted that the company could not guarantee against further layoffs. Steelcase had two personnel reduction programs that were not quite as large in relation to the size of the company, but still the first in the company's history—and painful. Jeff Weber at Geo. E. Keith has used two-week plant shutdowns and reduced pay to avert layoffs, but he is constantly aware of the financial sacrifices the workers are making as he and his management team strive to turn the company around.

External Partnerships

Relationships with suppliers, vendors, and financial institutions have become more partnering than adversarial. Levi Strauss & Co. analyzes its business from the making of cloth to the retail sale of jeans. It has reduced its denim manufacturers from about a dozen to four or five closer relationships. Its finance and marketing professionals help retailers with their business. The LeviLink™ information system uses bar coding and electronic data interchange (EDI) to transmit information back to the factory on what sizes and styles have been sold every day, helping retailers stock the right merchandise while keeping total inventory to a minimum.

In sharing information and dealing with banks, Levi Strauss & Co. Treasurer Joe Maurer considers himself to be sitting on the same side of the table. A commercial or investment banker bringing a proprietary product idea to Levi Strauss & Co. can rest assured that it will not be shopped around to the competition. Avoiding surprises and maintaining credibility with banks and vendors is a survival strategy for Dave Harrington, treasurer at Geo. E. Keith.

Herman Miller is primarily an assembler, so component manufacturers are an integral part of its manufacturing chain. Some relationships go back more than a quarter century. Quality and reliability are more important than price, though Herman Miller does review suppliers' financials to understand things such as cost allocations.

Implementation Methods

Once a company has articulated its principles and values and thought about the types of behavior it would like to encourage, it must develop specific programs to make those concepts come alive. Examples of such programs include measures to attract a more diverse workforce, company stock ownership and profit sharing plans, hiring criteria and performance appraisal systems linked to an organization's principles and values, loosening up expense approval procedures, improving internal financial reports, and outsourcing. Most companies in the study have both cross-functional teams and teams within the finance function. Companies in the study are encouraging finance people to have a general management orientation and to work closely with line operating people as partners and consultants. Finance people are being assigned to brands and business units, to cross-functional teams, to teams to support large customers, and to ad hoc problem solving task forces. With the larger companies in the study, the finance function is essentially decentralized and matrix-managed, with only a few treasury functions such as cash management and foreign exchange exposure management centralized.

Behavioral Results

In every company in the survey, finance people have more of a general management than a functional specialist orientation. Influencing skills are important for finance people at Herman Miller and Silicon Graphics. Finance people must be able to deal with ambiguity in the team and group decision making environment at Herman Miller and W. L. Gore. At both companies, the number of finance people in relation to total sales is considerably lower than in most large corporations.

Hiring and Evaluation of Finance People

Having solid technical knowledge and skills is a given in all the case study companies, but having good interpersonal skills is more important than being a functional star. Both Corning and Herman Miller believe that if you want to be just a financial technician, you should work at another company. Silicon Graphics is looking for "all-around athletes" to become its managers and leaders in the future.

W. L. Gore and Herman Miller hire primarily for specific positions and recruit very few people directly from school.

Peer review is part of the evaluation process at W. L. Gore, Levi Strauss & Co., Herman Miller, and Silicon Graphics.

Each person in the company brings a unique set of gifts, skills, and experiences, according to the philosophy at W. L. Gore, Herman Miller, and Steelcase. Unless a person's weaknesses somehow interfere with his or her strengths and ability to contribute, W. L. Gore would rather just ignore the weaknesses.

Career Paths for Finance People

Career paths for finance people have more of a general management than a functional specialist orientation in the companies participating in this study. At Harley-Davidson, CEO Richard Teerlink emphasizes the importance of finance people getting into other areas for parts of their careers in order to understand what is going on in the real world. People often move from finance to general management positions at Corning and Herman Miller. Silicon Graphics is an exception because of its high-technology orientation; most of its business unit heads are electrical engineers.

Role of Finance Function in Cultural Change

Three of the nine case-study companies, Geo. E. Keith, Harley-Davidson, and Levi Strauss & Co., are LBOs (leveraged buyouts). The challenge of the LBO for Levi Strauss & Co., and outright financial difficulty for Geo. E. Keith and Harley-Davidson, have been catalysts for cultural change. Because of life-threatening financial pressure, the finance function played a predominant role. At Geo. E. Keith and Harley-Davidson, the CFO became the CEO. Terry Larsen, CEO of CoreStates, believes that the finance function would have a hard time as the initiator of cultural change in the organization. However, once top management has initiated the process, he believes that functions such as finance and human resources play a vital role because they administer processes that touch everyone in the organization.

Role of CEO in Cultural Change

At CoreStates, Corning, Levi Strauss & Co., and Silicon Graphics, the current CEO was the initiator of cultural change. At Silicon Graphics, the CEO has provided a culture in which people are comfortable with change and view it as an opportunity.

External Reaction to Cultural Change

Both Terry Larsen of CoreStates and Richard Teerlink of Harley-Davidson have found it difficult to get Wall Street analysts to understand the role of cultural change in the company's long-term strategic and financial outlook.

4

CoreStates Financial Corp

Interview Subjects: *Terrence A. Larsen, chairman and chief executive officer; David C. Carney, chief financial officer; Carol A. Leisenring, executive vice president and chief economist; Albert W. Mandia, executive vice president—Financial Division; David J. Martin, executive vice president and chief counsel; Jorge A. Leon, senior vice president—Mergers and Acquisitions*

Executive Summary

The CoreValues and the quality program are the very foundation for CoreStates Financial Corp's strategy to compete in the 1990s. The CoreValues were defined by the company's People Task Force after CEO Terry Larsen perceived an uneven culture among several newly merged institutions. The bank believes that a values-driven culture must be in place before a quality program can be successfully implemented. A diversity initiative has been the first major step in the cultural change process. Soft skills such as leading, coaching, counseling, and teamwork appear prominently on the list of performance appraisal criteria for finance and other professionals.

Larsen believes that functions such as finance and human resources are essential catalysts in cultural change because they interact with everyone in the organization. One way the finance function has demonstrated its commitment to cultural change is by loosening up capital expenditure and travel expense approval procedures.

The finance function at CoreStates has assigned liaison people to work day-to-day with line groups while maintaining a straight-line reporting relationship with the head of the Financial Division. Informal communication has improved. Finance people are involved from the beginning as decisions are being considered.

CoreStates has formed partnerships with other institutions to offer services. The bank believes that many different types of partnerships will be possible in the future, including selling services to and buying services from other financial institutions.

Background

CoreStates Financial Corp, based in Philadelphia, Pennsylvania, was the 32nd largest bank-holding company in the United States at the end of 1993, with consolidated assets of $23.7 billion. The holding company was originally formed by the Philadelphia National Bank and now includes First Pennsylvania Bank, also in Philadelphia; Hamilton National Bank of Lancaster, Pennsylvania; New Jersey National Bank of Pennington, New Jersey; and a number of smaller banks. Through First Pennsylvania, CoreStates traces its roots to the first commercial bank in the United States, the Bank of North America, founded in 1782.

Terrence Larsen, formerly the bank's chief economist, has been chief executive officer for six years. He has created a distinctive image for CoreStates by defining values and quality as the very foundation of its strategy. He decided to initiate a process of change after perceiving that the cultures of several banks recently combined into one institution were uneven and, in many respects, unhealthy.

The CoreValues

CoreStates' principles and values are wrapped into its six CoreValues:

- We value people. We will treat all people with respect and courtesy and create an environment that supports the attainment of their personal and professional aspirations.
- We value performance. Exceptional contributions by individuals and by teams are critical to CoreStates' successful perfor-

mance. Such contributions at all levels of the organization will be appreciated and recognized.

- We value diversity. We will actively promote an atmosphere of mutual respect for each other's differences, recognizing that our diversity creates a breadth of perspectives which strengthens our organization.
- We value teamwork. Teamwork is critical to our success. Trust and mutual respect for each other's responsibilities, functions, skills, and experience are essential ingredients of teamwork.
- We value communication. Open, candid communication flowing in all directions will be the norm. We emphasize that listening is a critical component of the communication process.
- We value integrity. We will strive to be recognized as an organization of the highest ethical standards and unquestioned integrity.

Recognizing the Need for Cultural Change

The CoreValues themselves are a product of a team effort. They are one result of management's recognition several years ago that a cultural change was needed. Terry Larsen, CEO, explains that when the bank started the cultural change process, there had been a number of changes in the organization, including key executives retiring and the acquisition of other institutions with different cultures and subcultures. After being CEO for a couple of years, Larsen observed a culture that was quite variable across the organization, healthy in some respects, unhealthy in others, but far from ideal. He met with groups of about a dozen employees a couple of times each month and observed a feeling of pressure and tension. A lot of people did not feel good about coming to work; it was a burden. There was clearly a problem. Larsen did not know the answer, but he knew that something had to be done.

Human Resources was working on the edge of the problem, but something more was required. They needed some kind of catalyst to create more of an overall change and a real break from the past. Larsen asked the chief credit policy officer, in whom he had a great deal of confidence, to shift gears and assume responsibility for what became known as the People Task Force. Larsen defined the overall outcomes that he wanted but left the rest up to the task force. The task force in turn reached out and involved some existing groups, such as an informal senior women's group, that were trying to make a difference in the organization.

The People Task Force conducted a companywide survey to get an understanding of how employees viewed their work environment and the corporate culture, and where they felt there were problems. This input helped the task force to define the CoreValues. Now, two years later, the task force's original mission has been accomplished and it is folding itself into a new leadership circle. A new companywide survey was planned for fall 1993 to revisit some of the issues in the first survey and gauge the progress that has been made.

Diversity Initiative

CoreStates decided that a diversity initiative would be the first major step in the cultural change process, because of diversity's recognized importance and efforts that were already underway and going well. Not only did diversity issues underlie some of the morale problems, but the bank recognized how demographics were changing the composition of workforce. Two-thirds of its employees are women, and 26 percent are minorities.

Efforts underway to increase diversity awareness included the informal senior women's group and a diversity training program. The bank hired an outside consultant to hold diversity training seminars and has been very happy with the results, in contrast to empowerment seminars delivered by another consultant that have not been as well received.

In the seminars, managers are reminded that diversity has a broad meaning, encompassing not just race and gender but also differences in sexual orientation; dual-income families; single parents; and divorced, married, and single people. The bank must deal with this entire spectrum of people and be sensitive to all of their personal needs if it is to make a successful investment in its people. The seminars help people understand some of their own basic attitudes and assumptions. For example, white males have had the advantage of deference all their lives because of their race and their gender. They have been considered natural leaders, and the table has been tilted toward them. David Carney, CFO, says, "We are not going to implement and monitor quotas; that's unfair to the white males. We're not going to tilt the playing field; we're just going to level it. Not keeping it level could kill the entire enterprise." He believes that such a mutual understanding is necessary to attract and retain the best people and is imperative before the bank takes on additional steps such as empowerment. In his opinion, "It is difficult to have an open mind about empowerment if you have a prejudiced position toward minorities."

Each member of the bank's senior management has had at least three days of off-site training; David Carney has had five. Carney has worked with each unit reporting to him to develop a diversity action plan, and has drawn up a game plan for the entire finance function to foster a better working environment and a more level playing field that will allow people to prosper.

Role of the Finance Function in Cultural Change

Terry Larsen, CEO, believes that the finance function has an important role in the corporate cultural change effort. If the organization is trying to be more empowering and to get decision making closer to the customer, the financial area with all of its controls and potential rigidity can either be a catalyst for change or can slow things down. The bank has tried to use the human resources and finance areas as catalysts at the early stage of the cultural change process. Both areas affect large numbers of people and are fairly centralized. Changes made in these areas become obvious to a lot of people and help deliver the message throughout the organization that the bank views the process of creating a new culture very seriously.

While acknowledging the key role of the finance function in the cultural change process, Larsen believes that it would be very difficult for the finance function to initiate cultural change independently without the support of the CEO and the organization at large. Because the finance function works with everyone else, it would be constantly running into opposite behaviors. And Larsen points out that even when the CEO and the top management group are aligned, bringing about cultural change is not easy.

Time Required for Cultural Change

When CoreStates started the cultural change process, executives who had been successful at changing the cultures of other organizations told Larsen that it was at least a five-year process and could be closer to ten. CoreStates is now two and a half years into the process, and it is clear to Larsen that it will be a five- to ten-year process even though the bank is seeing signs that it is working and people are convinced that the program is not going to go away.

Total Quality Management and Cultural Change

The bank recently initiated a TQM program that is a focal point of its plans to compete with other banks and nonbank competitors such as mutual funds. It is spearheaded by the former chief credit policy officer and a senior vice president. TQM programs are now widespread in banking and throughout the American economy. Such a program was a particularly good fit for CoreStates because of the importance and good reputation of its nonloan operating services. How people treat their internal customers is often considered an important part of TQM, and some companies may go so far as to consider their principles and values as a subset of TQM. David Carney believes that the bank's CoreValues and cultural change must be in place already for a TQM program to be successful. But in the long run, he thinks that the TQM program will be a good laboratory in which to test the corporation's success in implementing its CoreValues.

Financial Liaison in Business Units

The establishment of financial liaison people in business units is an important example of empowerment and teamwork at CoreStates. The bank had a complex matrix management system in the past. In reevaluating the system, it considered the benefits of centralizing staff support functions or pushing them into the business groups. The finance and human resources functions allowed a compromise; they could be administered centrally, but a number of their people could be assigned to work with the business groups. Financial liaison groups are assigned to each business group such as wholesale banking, retail banking, and trust; to a number of the support areas such as human resources; and to affiliate banks such as New Jersey National and

CoreStates Bank of Delaware. The size of the liaison group varies from about five to 20 people depending on the size of the business group it supports.

Albert Mandia, executive vice president and Financial Division head, foresees a time when the wholesale banking, retail banking, and trust business groups and their financial liaison groups will serve all of the banks in the holding company. For example, consolidation of the functions of Hamilton Bank in Lancaster with those of the Philadelphia banks reduced annual expenses by $800,000 for the corporation, $600,000 of which was related to the finance function. But because units such as New Jersey National Bank cannot be consolidated with the Pennsylvania banks as one legal entity, there must still be some costly duplication of capabilities.

The liaison groups have a straight-line reporting relationship with Mandia and a dotted-line relationship with the business groups. The financial liaison people are housed with the business groups, and their day-to-day priorities come from the business groups. They know that their primary responsibility is to service their customers. They are empowered to make decisions related to the businesses they support, but if those decisions have a potential impact on CoreStates as a whole, they consult Mandia.

Mandia meets with the financial group heads once a week to discuss priorities, problems, and broader issues, and he maintains informal contact on a day-to-day basis as well. All the financial liaison people are hired by Financial. Mandia makes recommendations on the person to head each liaison group and does performance appraisals with input from the business groups. Sometimes business group heads recommend bonuses for financial liaison people working with them, but Mandia must maintain equity among the financial liaison people working for all the business groups. In addition, the financial liaison person's accomplishments for the business group are partly the result of people in the back office, who must also be fairly compensated.

When the financial liaison groups were established, their first mission was to demonstrate to their host groups that they added value. They demonstrated the benefits of one-stop shopping. People in the business groups could go to one person in the liaison group for any internal financial concern such as loan accounting, purchasing, accounts payable, and so forth. By knowing the back office staff and being recognized by them as a customer, the liaison person could expedite operations and save the business group people from having to call purchasing or accounts payable separately.

The finance function is involved at the earliest stages when the business groups are making decisions, rather than after the fact as in the past. For example, when CoreStates sold its Australian commercial finance company to State Street, the finance people were involved at an early stage, doing financial analysis and demonstrating a number of alternatives that CoreStates might have, such as downsizing versus selling. The Financial Division was brought in to the decision to downsize the bank's London operation at an early stage, and was involved from the beginning in the decision to buy a third-party lockbox processing business.

Fifteen years ago, the Financial Division was seen as the recorder. The business groups made decisions, and finance people found out after the fact and made sure the accounting was done properly. Now, finance people are considered part of the business group team—people who try to figure out a way to do things rather than saying why they can't be done. There is more informal communication between finance people and line people. When the job grades for people supporting businesses were evaluated recently, five of the six business group heads described the liaison part of the decision making process and the strategic thought process.

Hiring and Performance Criteria for the Financial Division

Al Mandia considers himself a people person more than a technician. Beyond the requisite technical skills, he looks for people who can get along with others and get things done through people. These characteristics, along with written and oral communication skills, are crucial for people in financial liaison positions.

The performance appraisal criteria (figure 6) for financial liaison people cover supporting the businesses, training and developing team members, working as a team with financial division colleagues, being sensitive to people values such as diversity, and getting things done on time. Meeting deadlines is particularly important in the financial planning process because business group plans must be consolidated centrally before an overall corporate plan is presented to the board.

FIGURE 6: Performance Appraisal Criteria

Performance Skills: Managerial

Planning: Forecasts relevant operating and business conditions; establishes appropriate objectives, strategies, and action plans; effectively budgets capital and operating resources.

Organizing: Develops and communicates an efficient, well-understood organization appropriate to business goals and requirements; considers limitations, talents, availability, and interests of people; effectively delegates authority to subordinates to enable them to carry out responsibilities.

Leading: Leads and influences employees to accomplish business goals and objectives; gains credibility and respect from peers and subordinates; maintains effective upward and downward communications; develops employees' skills and potential.

Coaching and Counseling: Develops performance standards to measure achievement of plans and objectives; effectively measures performance results; identifies deviations from standards and takes appropriate corrective actions.

Human Resource Utilization: Ensures that all employees are treated in a fair and equitable manner; develops human resource plans to meet anticipated organizational needs and enhance individual growth; strives to meet affirmative action goals; fully complies with established personnel policies and procedures.

Performance Skills: Professional

Sales/Account Management: Establishes and maintains effective business relationships with present and potential customers; recognizes and develops business opportunities within established pricing and profitability standards; identifies and refers prospective customers for other products/services; effectively coordinates efforts with other bank resources and uses them to maximize sales results; demonstrates effective selling skills to negotiating/closing techniques; understands and integrates customer needs and business/profit objectives.

Project Management: Effectively manages unit resources to minimize expense and maximize results; monitors and communicates project status and takes necessary remedial action; effectively utilizes other bank resources to achieve results.

Technical Knowledge: Applies knowledge and abilities gained through training and experience to performance of job; keeps informed of new developments in his or her field and provides relevant information to others.

Staff Support: Contributes to the effectiveness of line departments by providing support services in a responsive manner; shows initiative in anticipating user needs and developing appropriate programs/services; effectively manages conflicting user demands.

FIGURE 6: Performance Appraisal Criteria (continued)

Performance Skills: Personal

People Are at the Core of CoreStates: Strives to make CoreStates a caring and vital place to work, with a strong sense of family, trust, support, team spirit, respect, and courtesy.

Problem Solving: Effectively identifies/analyzes problems, develops alternative approaches, and solves the problems.

Judgment and Decision Making: Shows ability to obtain relevant information; exercises discretion and sound judgment; shows decisiveness in taking or recommending action.

Interpersonal Skills: Demonstrates tact, diplomacy, and the ability to direct, influence, and work cooperatively with others.

Time Management: Effectively manages own time by establishing priorities and developing work plans/schedules.

Managing Conflict: Demonstrates the ability to maintain composure and productivity under adverse operating conditions, conflicts and pressures.

Communication/Presentation Skills: Exhibits effective oral and written communications in terms of format and organization, clarity and conciseness, understanding of audience, and ability to sell ideas.

Teamwork: Works effectively with others to achieve overall team results; shows willingness to actively take part or lead group efforts; resolves group conflicts in a productive manner.

Adaptability: Shows ability to respond/adjust quickly and smoothly to changing conditions.

Training and Development in the Finance Function

Counseling and coaching team members is an important responsibility of senior financial liaison people. Other training for team members includes an overall corporate orientation program, personnel development and management training courses, and specialized seminars on subjects such as handling conflict. There are task forces on career planning and development and customer service within the finance group.

Career Opportunities

The finance function has a wide span of control that allows for a variety of career opportunities. There is a job posting system for internal staff movement. Aside from its traditional financial reporting and tax responsibilities, the finance function has system projects and other operational functions such as loan accounting, purchasing, accounts payable, and records retention. Good managers are always in demand.

There are opportunities to move between the finance function and other areas of the bank. Auditing, for example, provides a useful background for people moving into the finance function because of its necessary contact with all phases of bank operations. Finance people find opportunities in other parts of the bank as well—for example the wholesale bank training program and the product management group. Al Mandia likes to make sure that those opportunities are real career changes and not just attempts by business groups to create their own finance functions.

Service Versus Control

Traditionally, the role of the Financial Division has been control. Two years ago, a group of senior managers in the division debated just who they were, and whether they were a service function or a control function. The business groups were interested more in service, but the bank still needed controls. A balance was required. The Financial Division has attempted to make processes more user friendly and to eliminate levels of approval. It has tried to put in place policies and procedures that minimize the requirement for finance people to act as policemen. In today's environment such a role makes everyone uncomfortable, particularly younger staff members.

Process Improvement Teams

The bank started to implement the team concept through process improvement teams. Eight prototype teams were coordinated by Carol Leisenring, chief economist, who is in charge of the bank's strategic planning, chairs its Asset and Liability Management Committee, and also chaired the Empowerment Task Force. The teams were coached by Ernst & Young Consultants. The teams selected projects with a high likelihood of success. This was not because they were trying to sell the concept—people had already bought it—but so they could train people with manageable projects and allow people to grow in what they could do.

Managers had to learn a new role. They were counseled not to try to direct the teams or ask for weekly progress reports, but to let the team members do the work and develop the recommendations.

Each team has come up with 70 or 80 recommendations, and managers have bought most of the ideas in the team reports. The acceptance rate has been about 95 percent.

The prototype teams have served as a model for additional teams. David Carney, CFO, estimates that there are numerous other teams in the bank organized on a more ad hoc basis, without formal expertise or leadership. He says, "This is a process we could not stop if we tried."

The way the Loan Accounting/Transportation and Equipment Task Force solved a problem with duplication of effort illustrates how an informal process improvement team works.

By their very nature, secured loans for airplanes, leasing, and trucking companies have complex documentation. To protect the bank's secured position and to provide quick and responsive turnaround for customer requests, it is important for the loan officer to know that all the required documents are on hand, recorded, and accessible. For years the lending officers and the Loan Accounting Documentation Unit had been mired down with layer upon layer of procedures, checking and rechecking work. Redundancies had developed between the two groups, but it was difficult for people to sit down together to resolve the problems, because each area only knew their own piece of the credit granting process.

A former lending officer, now in charge of the Loan Accounting Department, assembled a team from both that group and the line unit to address the documentation workflow issues. The team developed 23 recommendations on how things could be done differently. Shortly thereafter, the head of the Transportation and Equipment Group raved about the improvement in the bank's Management Committee meeting.

Capital Expenditures and Travel Expenses

The Financial Division's simplification of capital expenditure and travel expense approval procedures has had both practical and symbolic impact. In the past, there was resentment that the Financial Division was trying to mind everybody's business and control too much. The division had restricted the ability of people in the organization to act, for example in buying equipment, opening new branches, or starting new businesses. The bank's officers were affected personally by a very restrictive travel and expense policy. CFO Carney said, "Coming from the collegial atmosphere of a Big Six accounting firm, I thought that if I'm going to take somebody's lunch hour to talk business, at least I can buy lunch." The chairman admitted that even he felt restricted. The bank rewrote and opened up the travel and expense policy so that people could do things they thought were appropriate.

The bank uses authorization for capital expenditure (AFE) forms for capital items and major marketing programs. The Financial Division reduced the levels of approval from three to one, setting an example for the business groups to simplify their approval processes in the same way. In some cases, an officer's AFE-signing authority has been increased tenfold, from $25,000 to $250,000. The dollar level of AFEs that required approval by the chairman or the board was increased. Now a relatively small number of items, most of them over $5,000,000, require approval at that level.

Approval processes for invoices and expenditures have been made more user friendly. Senior vice presidents no longer need their bosses to sign off on magazine subscriptions. Lower level signatures are required for expenses that are within the approved plan, and a higher level is required for those outside the plan.

Impressed accounts for cash disbursements have been created for the business groups. They can spend money, send in documentation for the money they have spent, and then get more. This has given the business groups more authority for small expenditures and reduced the paperwork for the accounts payable group. The business groups are responsible for reconcilement, subject to review by the Financial Division.

Exploring the Boundaries of Empowerment

Carol Leisenring believes that the bank is still exploring and learning what empowerment really means. Some financial processes actually appear contradictory to empowerment. The bank's asset and liability management system permits business managers considerable latitude, for example, in pricing loans and deposits. Delegating asset and liability management is difficult because the process is highly detailed and not fully understood in the business units. For example, many lending officers don't understand that transfer pricing for a loan includes a premium for prepayment risk that should be passed on to the customer. Lending officers may be upset when they can only offer interest-rate caps at a price premium over the competition, but they may not understand how much risk a cap puts on the bank's balance sheet. The Asset and Liability Management Group (ALCO) is trying to help the business units understand the process. The message they are conveying is, "Don't assume you can't do it. Come to us; talk to us; explain why this is an issue for you. Maybe we can work something out, or help you understand why the situation exists." Slowly, the communication process is improving.

Bank Acquisitions: Teamwork and Concern with Culture

Teamwork and a concern with the culture of a potential merger candidate are part of the way of doing business in the bank's mergers and acquisitions function, headed by Jorge Leon, senior vice president. Terry Larsen started the group two years ago to help implement his vision that the industry was consolidating and that the government would encourage strong institutions like CoreStates to buy weak and failing ones. Leon believes that the bank is positioned to be a successful acquirer because of its good financial condition, profitability, and established service quality. He believes that these qualities will make CoreStates more successful than other bank-holding companies that are using acquisitions as the engine of their growth.

A full-time team of four continually screens merger candidates, analyzing their financial condition and assessing whether they would be a good strategic and cultural fit. When the bank decides to perform due diligence or actually acquire another bank, it draws from other functions to create ad hoc task forces. A due diligence task force includes human resources people who evaluate the target's culture and management style. In checking out a number of institutions, task force members have continually refined their checklist and their visceral analysis capability. The human resources people talk to various members of management and supplement their own observations by talking to the 50 to 60 other members of the due diligence team about what they have seen, heard, and learned.

Some mergers have not been pursued because there was a fundamental difference between the two cultures and the target was large enough to have an impact. For example, the managements of some candidates have seemed to be autocratic and non-employee oriented, or to possess substantially different business philosophies. An autocratic management or a period of financial difficulty affects the attitudes of employees. The human resources team has to evaluate whether these kinds of problems are insurmountable, or, if CoreStates goes through with the acquisition, how they can be solved.

After an agreement is signed, the bank establishes a merger integration task force in which all functions are represented. Implementing the culture is a process, not an event. Typically, it starts with a letter from Terry Larsen welcoming new people to the organization, saying what CoreStates is all about, and explaining the CoreValues. Often there is initial skepticism and cynicism about the CoreValues in light of expected staffing reductions. How decisions are implemented and how leaders and managers of CoreStates do their jobs after closing is an important way of communicating values to a new subsidiary. Open and honest communication is particularly important. It must be explained that no CoreValue says that unnecessary positions will not be eliminated. Where possible, the bank places people in new jobs through an in-placement program, taking advantage of people's training and saving severance pay. In one local savings bank acquisition, 280 jobs were eliminated, but only 17 people had to be outplaced.

In this business, Leon explains that there is little choice but to empower people. Barriers to empowerment are people who do not really want to empower other people, and people who do not truly want to be empowered, have responsibility, be held accountable, and take some personal risk. Team members at CoreStates are drawn from all levels within the organization. This small team has responsibility for a potential investment of hundreds of millions of dollars, acting as the bank's eyes, ears, and brains to evaluate whether the business, financial, and cultural fit makes sense. When team members are in a remote location, they do not have a lot of supervision. The bank is counting on them to do the job. They have to ask the right questions, see the right people, challenge the right assumptions, cover the ground they feel they need to cover, and bring back their honest opinions. Of course, Leon explains, the bank counts on its more talented, experienced, proactive people to do that kind of work. But the point is that there is no business choice but empowerment to get this kind of job done.

Organizational learning is an instrumental part of what the mergers and acquisitions function does. The group started with only limited experience two years ago. One of its first challenges was to increase the institutional and team learning in this area. Being active in the market has helped it do this. Each time the group has gone through the process of evaluating, performing due diligence, and consummating a deal, members have tried to learn together and to reformulate what they will try to do next time. A core group of people has been involved almost every time. They have learned what to look for and the questions to ask. The group is involving new people in the process so that they too can learn, and the bank gains flexibility in staffing. Jorge Leon says, "We are still learning institutionally, but in terms of how to bring a new organization into ours, we are light years ahead of where we were two years ago."

Partnerships with Other Financial Institutions

CoreStates is engaged in a number of joint ventures and strategic alliances with other financial institutions. Another bank may be a competitor, but it may become a joint venture partner at the same time. CoreStates has been a leader in developing point-of-sale, credit card, and automated teller machine (ATM) systems for its own use and for sale to other banks. CoreStates decided that the value of this business and its own financial objectives would be best served if another bank was brought in as a partner, and PNC Financial Corporation, BancOne Corporation, and Society Corporation are now co-owners of the business.

A group has been established to explore other businesses in which CoreStates can offer services to other banks, particularly where it can achieve a competitive advantage through economies of scale. CoreStates has acquired a third-party lockbox processor, capitalizing on its strong reputation for cash management services. In the future the bank may consider outsourcing the back-office operation of other products where it does not have such a competitive advantage or where potential volume does not warrant the necessary capital investment. The mergers and acquisitions team has no reservation about involving outside advisers when their expertise can add value.

The team may use real estate consultants as part of due diligence teams or investment bankers to advise on valuation, structuring, and negotiations. However, it is explained to them that they are joining a team, not running the process. CoreStates must take ultimate responsibility for the team effort because it will have to live with the decision.

The bank once explored making a joint bid for a financially troubled target bank, working with another bank acquiror and arranging to split the franchise. Leon thought that the joint bid could have given CoreStates a competitive advantage. Each party would have paid a premium only for the parts of the franchise it valued the most. He believes that the bid would have been time consuming and complicated, but it could have worked. CoreStates was comfortable with the culture of the other acquiror through a long-standing correspondent relationship. Unfortunately, the seller didn't care for such an approach.

CoreStates has also considered working with an investment banking firm to sell problematic or nonstrategic assets that it doesn't want, packaging and selling them in the securities market.

Broadening the Understanding of CoreValues

Carol Leisenring believes that the majority of people in the organization think about the CoreValues in terms of treating people fairly, communicating with them, and developing them, but not as much in relation to their day-to-day "hard" business responsibilities. The systems person has not thought very much about how the CoreValues affect a systems project. An ALCO liaison person may be fully comfortable with the need to go to the retail banking group to discuss a pricing issue, but probably has not yet thought conceptually about the connection between the CoreValues and the need for dialogue to resolve business problems.

Getting people outside the organization, such as security analysts, to understand the potential benefit to the business of the CoreValues is a challenge too. In the beginning, David Carney's discussion of the CoreValues and how they related to the strategy of the corporation was treated as a distraction. Though the analysts did not go so far as to say the company should not be doing these things, they did not want to hear any more about them. They were interested in hearing about the traditional kinds of activities, the day-to-day numbers and the company's strategies in each of its businesses and markets. The CoreValues initiative was launched in a recession and a time of heavy credit losses in the industry, and the analysts were worried that attention may have been diverted from credit quality. Some felt that if they recommended the stock on this basis, they would have lost their jobs before the impact was reflected on the bottom line. Now, two years later, the analysts are paying more attention to the CoreValues for several reasons. The bank reinforced its credibility by coming through the credit-loss period in good shape. Larsen appointed Chuck Coltman, formerly chief credit policy officer and well known and respected by the analysts, as head of the bank's quality program. Finally, the analysts have grown more comfortable with concepts such as corporate values over time. Larsen says, "Maybe we're explaining it and tying the elements together more effectively."

Keeping the Momentum Going

David Carney, CFO, believes that the biggest challenge in implementing the CoreValues is to keep momentum going. Terry Larsen, CEO, realizes that plenty of organizations have not succeeded in cultural change initiatives—even with objectives that appeared to make sense. "You don't automatically get there. You put the organization at risk when you make a culture change. But if we're successful, this will give us a competitive advantage." Larsen disagrees with any analyst who believes that the CoreValues and quality are not having an impact on the bottom line. He points out that people feel better about coming to work and that this comes through to customers, and in all of the things the bank does. Through the diversity initiative, the bank has reached out to all of its employees and said that it wants to support them and make them successful. This makes them feel good.

Two or three hundred people in upper management used to make all of the bank's decisions. Now most of them would at least intellectually agree that the bank needs to get decision making out nearer to the customer. Though some people have been against change, or said, "OK, but not in my area," Larsen says, "Ninety-eight percent of the organization is in favor of what we're trying to do. But it's still a long, hard process. We have a lot of training to do." He points out that if people are given authority to make decisions without the proper tools, they will not make good decisions. The bank has to go at a measured pace, giving people the training and confidence that they need to start making decisions, but also recognizing that some people don't want to make decisions, preferring to keep life simple as it has been and to just do as they are told.

Terry Larsen is optimistic. He concluded the interview by saying, "I'm very pleased with the way it is working."

5
Corning

Interview subjects: *Van C. Campbell, vice chairman; Richard B. Klein, senior vice president and controller; James B. Flaws, assistant treasurer; Alan T. Eusden, senior financial manager, Specialty Materials Group; Jack C. Simpson, manager, Administrative Operations and Services*

Executive Summary

Corning has been ahead of its time in much of the management thinking covered in this study. When James R. Houghton became CEO in 1983, he and his new Management Committee developed a set of values including quality, integrity, and respect for the individual. The company has been cited in a number of studies for its efforts to hire and promote women and minorities. Corning has more experience with joint ventures and strategic alliances than any major corporation.

Corning also has a lot of experience with teams throughout its plants and offices. In each business group and business unit, there are finance teams and there is a finance person working as part of the team reporting to the general manager. Since 1989, a number of finance functions such as payroll, accounts payable, and accounts receivable have been the responsibility of self-managed teams in Corning's Administration Center.

Empowerment and self-managed teams have helped individuals at all levels improve their self-confidence and communication skills. Authority and responsibility have been pushed down to individuals and teams most qualified to make decisions. As capital budgeting and other decisions are made at lower levels, layers of management are starting to become unnecessary. Empowerment is not inconsistent with control as long as people understand why controls are needed, and that measures such as separation of duties within teams are not a reflection on their own integrity.

In hiring and evaluating finance professionals, Corning looks for well-rounded people with good interpersonal skills and a general management orientation. Being a cooperative and useful member of a finance or cross-functional team can be as important as technical capability. Finance people at Corning often move on to general management positions.

Background

Corning began as a glassmaker in Brooklyn. In 1868, Amory Houghton, supported by local investors, moved the company to Corning, New York. His great great grandson, James R. Houghton—known as Jamie—heads the company today. The company has long been known for consumer products such as Corning Ware, Revere Ware, Pyrex ovenproof glass, and Steuben crystal. In the past decade, Jamie has spearheaded the company's move into higher growth and higher margin businesses such as specialty materials (ceramic materials for emission control devices, automobile and industrial lamps, and scientific lab ware), communications (optical fibers), and laboratory services (clinical testing for doctors, hospitals, food processors, and pharmaceutical manufacturers). Having a substantial portion of the company's stock in friendly hands, including those of employees and the Houghton family, has helped Jamie Houghton focus on building business over a longer term. Corning has an employee stock purchase plan.

Defining Company Values

When Houghton became CEO in 1983, he formed the Management Committee, including himself and five others. He wanted to make sure that everyone on that committee knew and agreed on what the company stood for. This was an unusual opportunity because the new

CEO and the Management Committee were starting at the same time. A lengthy debate on the company's values ensued.

The Management Committee agreed on seven values:

- Quality
- Integrity
- Performance
- Leadership
- Technology
- Independence
- Valuing the individual

Quality

Quality was the first value that the Management Committee defined, years ahead of the TQM movement we hear so much about today. The committee members didn't all know exactly what it meant, but they knew it was important. They learned that part of quality is identifying who the customers are and what they want. A lot of customers are internal. This was a new concept for the finance function.

The biggest obstacle in getting the quality movement started was the opinion inside the company, "We've always done quality work." That was generally considered to be true, but one had to ask, "How do you know?" and "How can you measure it?" Another problem was that some of the easiest things to measure were not necessarily the most important.

Integrity

When financial officers at Corning discuss values, integrity stands out above the others. At the time the values were defined, the controller said, "Integrity is the bottom line." Van Campbell, vice chairman for Finance and Administration, recalling the process, says, "We had always considered ourselves the guardians of financial and legal integrity and corporate reputation, so that one really played."

Jim Flaws, assistant treasurer, says, "Integrity pervades everything we do. Top management of the company walks this value, and that is one of the reasons I am still with the company after 20 years."

The finance function is viewed within Corning as a bastion of integrity, and in that light it is sometimes called to arbitrate disputes within the company. For example, two Corning general managers once made separate promises to corporate partners in different joint ventures that turned out to be 180 degrees apart in impact. The general managers were unable to resolve the dispute. A decision was made to let the two respective group financial managers develop a fair solution that would consider the interests of both Corning and its joint venture partners. The solution to the problem was complex because the joint venture partners were located in France and Mexico. The financial managers' solution was accepted by the Corning general managers and the joint venture partners. As another example of integrity, when the Foreign Corrupt Practices Act was introduced in the early 1980s, Corning reviewed its internal procedures and found that they were tighter than the government requirements. The company's financial function continues to maintain regulations that are stricter than legally required.

Performance

Corning could not be one of the world's great companies without good financial performance. Despite the importance of the softer values, this basic objective remained a top priority.

Leadership

The company wants to be a leader in everything it does, but leadership means being the best at doing what customers say they need, not necessarily being at the technological leading edge in every one of the company's businesses.

Technology

The company wants to achieve leadership through technical innovation and linking specific expertise with market needs.

Valuing the Individual

The company knows that in the end the commitment and contribution of all its employees will determine its success. Corning believes in the fundamental dignity of the individual. Its network consists of a rich mixture of people of diverse nationality, race, gender, and opinion. The company believes that this will continue to be a source of strength. It values the unique ability of each individual to contribute and intends that every employee shall have the opportunity to participate fully, grow professionally, and develop to his or her highest potential. There are about 700 people in the finance and administrative areas, and developing, nurturing, promoting, and diversifying applies to this area as well as every other in the company.

Empowerment

Jim Flaws, assistant treasurer, defines empowerment as stripping away levels of approval that may have nothing to do with where the true work is being done and where the impact is really being felt. He believes that what is usually missing when someone talks about empowerment is some measure of accountability and responsibility. In the past, the company had many layers of approval, but people who were meant to be accountable and responsible did not really know enough about what they were approving—whether something was really needed in the business, whether something was the right thing to do. Today, the company is trying to push accountability down along with power.

Credit Decision Making in Business Units

Flaws cites the example of credit decision making, centered mostly in accounts receivable in the past. This group made credit decisions with no knowledge of Corning's business relationship with the customer. Now people managing businesses and people with sales responsibility are involved in the credit decision-making process. In the past, there was a centralized reserve for credit losses, and businesses did not "take the hit." Now, if people make wrong credit decisions, the resulting losses will be charged to their divisions.

One Person Responsible for Commercial Paper Borrowing

Today, a person one step above the clerical level manages cash and makes commercial paper borrowing decisions for the corporation. In the past, more people were involved. The person might have consulted her boss, who in turn might have gone to see an assistant treasurer such as Jim Flaws. If she had done her job properly, there was no reason for Flaws to tell her she couldn't borrow the money. It was unrealistic for him to continually review her work papers. Time was better spent making sure she was qualified to do the job and was performing well.

Eliminating Layers of Management

Van Campbell, Vice Chairman for Finance and Administration, believes that the company can't just decide to empower everybody without walking them through total quality, teamwork, and all of the requirements of their jobs. Only then can it feel comfortable allowing people to manage their own affairs, knowing that they know what they are expected to deliver.

Campbell believes that as empowerment and self-managed teams spread through the company, layers of management will be eliminated. "People are on teams, making recommendations, solving problems. They ask, 'What does he do? Why do we need a boss? We figured all this out.' And there isn't a good answer. When you push the responsibility down to the level where teams are interacting with customers, you eventually take out layers of management because there isn't much for them to do."

Pushing Down Spending Authority

The capital budgeting process is being pushed down to division and plant managers. Spending authority is being increased at all levels. Business units are developing capital budgets consistent with their strategic plans, justifying expenditures by their effect on ROE (return on equity). Campbell sees about 10 to 20 percent of the appropriation requests (ARs). Most of them are over $5 million. The Office of the Chairman concentrates on the half-dozen proposals that are really going to make a strategic difference to the company.

Goal of Self-Management

Campbell believes that self-management is the ultimate empowerment, and that people at Corning today feel more empowered than they used to. The organization has been slimmed down. More people are able to make presentations to him and to Jamie Houghton. People at lower levels are more confident in making decisions on their own because they believe they have the necessary information, and they sense that there are clearer criteria for what is important and how their performance is measured. What was perceived as a class, hierarchical system seems to have been modified.

Empowerment and TQM

Empowerment has been reinforced by the company's total quality management program. Every person is meant to own a process or part of a process and directly influence key results indicators (KRIs). People can see the results of their performance on computer-generated TQM charts, produced in bold color and displayed in the hallways.

Control and Empowerment

Campbell does not see a conflict between control and empowerment in a team environment. Most types of fraud require a conspiracy, and if two people on a team collude, other team members will notice it. Normally, a conspiracy requires two people in different organizations or at different levels. He believes business success comes from good decisions, not rigid budgets and tight controls. The best method of control is to have good people running businesses and to make your expectations clear.

Benefits and Problems with Self-Managed Teams

Campbell believes that teams have fostered communication and trust among people at all levels. Just about everybody has become a good personal communicator as a result of working on teams. People learn how to explain to others how they feel and what their problems are—skills that do not come easily for many people. They learn how to lead teams and how to make presentations.

Management helps this process by having coffee klatches with cross sections of people that include older, newer, and minority employees. In a friendly atmosphere, they are encouraged to talk about what is on their minds and what people are concerned about in their organizations and in the company as a whole. Campbell says, "We just open ourselves up. 'I'm not going to tell anybody who told me. Let's talk.' We are very open and trusting."

The biggest problem with empowered teams seems to be stress. Managers used to make all the decisions, evaluate employees, and give them feedback. Now, if a decision has to be made, the team has to make it. Team members have to work out problems on their own. Supervisors step in only when teams are spinning their wheels and really need help. Now feedback comes from team members, though they do not give each other actual performance evaluations. The supervisor consolidates feedback from all team members and uses that in reviewing performance with the individual.

Organizational Learning: Commitment to Training

Several years ago, CEO Jamie Houghton set an objective that 5 percent of everyone's time be spent in training. Corning has a core set of courses for everybody, and each person also works out a training plan with his or her supervisor. Training plans are set up to focus on the individual's relative weaknesses, either functional skills or general management skills that apply to any function, or training that someone needs to advance to the next job. Attending courses with people in other functions is helpful for getting to know more people within the company, but the company has found it effective for functional teams to attend courses as units. In this way, people who work with each other every day can take an opportunity to work on a live problem, or cite a live problem as an example in the class.

External Partnerships: Corning's Experience with Joint Ventures

More than one-third of Corning's earnings come from joint ventures of some kind, including partnerships and equity investments shared with other companies. Corning has had perhaps more experience than any other major corporation with joint ventures and strategic alliances. Since its first alliance—making cardboard boxes with Charles Rohm Company in 1924—Corning has been involved in more than 48 joint ventures. Today, Corning has a fifty-fifty share or a minority position in 20 ventures in 30 countries. The company's reasons for entering into joint ventures have included sharing risks and benefiting from the other party's expertise and technology while concentrating on what Corning does best. Joint ventures have allowed Corning in many cases to develop new products and to move into new markets more quickly and cheaply than it could by going alone.

Team Learning at Corning Vitro

Jim Flaws was responsible for creating Corning Vitro Corporation. It was his idea to form the joint venture, and he became the CFO. To create the corporate accounting department, Flaws formed a team. Then with that team he visited two other joint ventures, Corning Asahi Video and Ciba Corning Diagnostics, to see how they had set up their own accounting operations and what had worked well or poorly. One team learning together from another team with similar responsibilities was a new training experience—more effective than sending just one person.

Understanding the Partner

In developing and maintaining relationships with a partner, Corning tries to understand the partner's culture, its financial policies, and how it approaches decisions. In one case, the financial structure of a joint venture was the responsibility of just two people, Flaws and his counterpart in the other company. They spent a lot of time getting to know each other and just talking about things. Flaws explains that partnership and negotiating to protect your own interests need not be a contradiction. Corning has developed the philosophy that if one partner wins unfairly over the other in the negotiation, then the partnership will probably not work. It has learned through experience that if you do not look out for your partner's interests as well as your own, it will probably come back to haunt you.

Flaws recounts a recent example in a partnership when an unrecorded contingent liability came due. It was related to an event within Corning that took place before the joint venture was set up. Nothing would have prevented Flaws from booking the charge to the joint venture, but he knew that it would not be fair to the partner. Corning took the charge.

Flaws explains, "We're always trying to work with our partners on financial structure, planning, debt levels, dividends, how much freedom the joint venture should have in matters such as borrowing, whether it should borrow at all, or whether the parents should downstream funds." In matters such as dividends, Corning usually has an idea of the payout ratio it would like and tries to establish policies at the outset to avoid future disputes. But partners may have different cash needs, different philosophies about when to harvest cash and when to reinvest, and different tax rules. In one case, Corning's partner approached the general manager of a joint venture with a request to deviate from the policy and raise the dividend because of cash needs. The general manager asked Flaws to help determine why Corning should or should not go along with the higher dividend, what the implications were, and how to work with the partner to reach a mutually acceptable solution. Flaws gave the general manager a series of pluses and minuses on how to approach the decision. A decision was made to maintain a constant dividend policy and to declare a special dividend for that year. The partners also agreed that a special dividend could be considered by the joint venture's board in any year.

Another joint venture needed substantial new investment. Corning's partner said it did not care if it ever got a dividend, but it was never going to put in another dollar. It was not politically feasible to approach the partner's board for an additional investment in the joint venture. In contrast, Corning's policy was for joint ventures to pay dividends on a more regular basis and then to reinvest when necessary. Mindful of the partners' different financial policies, management of the joint venture had to anticipate the rainy day when it would really need investment dollars. Flaws has met with the partner's finance person to discuss the problem. This was more a problem for the finance people of the partners than for the finance people of the joint venture itself.

Financial Institution Relationships: A TQM Approach

Corning has annual relationship meetings every year with its primary commercial banks and investment banking firms. The institution's performance in the previous year is assessed, sometimes on a formal bank report card, sometimes just by a review of major transactions. Both parties review objectives and plans for the upcoming year. Corning applies total quality principles to the process, with special emphasis on mutual understanding of requirements, measuring performance, and developing processes to deliver the required results.

Importance of Soft Skills in Finance

Finance people at Corning must have an acceptable level of technical skills, but having good interpersonal skills is more important than being a technical superstar. Van Campbell allows that, in the past, people who went into the finance function may have had fewer interpersonal demands. But now in finance as well as every part of the company, managers' and workers' requirements have changed. The company is going to have an increasingly diverse workforce with tensions that must be managed and bridged. It has created expectations among all of its people about how they will be treated and how much they will be able to influence what goes on around them.

Campbell cites Dick Klein's management of the control function. "He treats them like real people, allows them to participate, values their judgments. Consequently, the effectiveness of that organization is incredible. Dick has also gotten good technical people. He has created a tremendously human atmosphere within that organization and given people a chance to grow. People come in with that kind of expectation. They do not just want to grind away at the numbers and work on their computers. They want to interact, work on teams, do the same thing everybody else does. This is caused by a combination of what they came with and the Corning culture."

Finance professionals at Corning appear not to have any difficulty in talking about the softer management concepts, and they appear to see no conflict between being a finance person and an empowered person. An important reason, according to Controller Dick Klein, is that they have been at it for 10 years. If the chairman had a different attitude, there might be more finance people who would find reasons that empowerment is not possible. Citing Houghton's three initiatives, performance, quality, and diversity, Klein says that a smart manager is going to do what the chairman wants. He adds, "If you really work at it, there is no conflict in any of this stuff. It doesn't conflict with good financial controls."

Campbell sees a generational change in business school graduates. "They were more like machines a generation ago—the McNamara school of whiz kids. Computers were just coming into being. Calculators. Net present value. We could analyze anything." He believes that there is a generational change that the company has to measure up to. If it doesn't, people are going to work someplace else. Today people are more concerned about each other and about feelings. They've had the benefit of their parents' financial success, so they're not as hungry or worried. Just the idea of making a living is not as driving a force as it was 30 years ago. Ranking at the top in school seems to be less important than taking a diversity of courses and being a balanced individual.

There are many more dual careers now. There is more sharing of the workload at home. Klein says that Corning tries not to schedule meetings after 5 p.m. because people have commitments such as picking up children from day care centers. This changes the way people feel about the balance in their lives. Klein says you have to be sensitive to that.

The balance between career and personal commitments also varies over time. People go through periods in their lives when they just can't work the way they used to—new mothers, for example—and then they might go back to that pace later.

Hiring

Corning's traditional approach to hiring in the past was to bring in people with little or no experience, and train and mold them as their careers progressed. Finance people started as analysts and assistant plant controllers. Now the approach is more eclectic. Some ABs and a greater number of MBAs are hired directly from school. An increasing number of new hires are now experienced, for example as CPAs.

Corning looks for well-rounded individuals with a general management orientation rather than functional superstars. When financial managers such as Alan Eusden recruit at college and business school campuses, they feel they can sell two important features: (1) Corning is hiring people for long-term careers; and (2) the company's focus is on having financial people as integral parts of business teams.

Finance Career Paths

Finance is a net exporting function. As the pyramid within finance starts to narrow, people can move into other functions. This is well accepted and encouraged. A number of people in the company in general management positions have a financial background. The general manager of Corning Asahi Video was previously the corporate controller. The manager of the Revere consumer product line was previously a division controller. This mobility provides the finance function with disciples out on the line and shows that people can move out from what is sometimes viewed as a narrow staff function.

Performance Evaluation and Career Planning

A senior management group of about 25 people, including the controller, treasurer, and their direct and indirect reports, reviews everybody in the finance function annually. They try to identify the professionals with the strongest potential, problem performers, and the needs of the function overall. This functional review builds on and is consistent with the individual's performance review with his or her supervisor.

Each person is placed within the performance appraisal matrix in figure 7.

FIGURE 7: Performance Appraisal Matrix

High Potential	Developing	New/Unknown
Strong Professional	Contributor	Concern

"High potential" is the grade assigned to top performers who have the potential to move up quickly. "Strong professionals" may not show as much potential for upward movement but are experienced and reliable. People who are "developing" may move up a few steps, but probably not to the top. Those marked "concern" do not show much potential for moving up. People do not always stay in the same place on the matrix. A person who was considered a "strong professional" last year may be considered "high potential" this year.

The management group considers the following for each person:

- Group number (based on responsibility and salary grade)
- Educational background
- How long the person has been in his/her present position
- Snapshot of strengths and weaknesses
- What the person wants to do
- The next best opportunity for the person (for example, a business controllership if there is an opening in the next six months or so)

Jobs are ranked by group numbers. The senior management group looks at the balance in the function. Are "high potentials" only in one job group number? How diverse are we? What is the level of turnover? How many people have been in their jobs less than 12 months? Should that frighten us? How does this compare to two or three years ago?

If the right opportunity arises for a person, the company tries not to hold him or her back for lack of an immediate replacement in his or her current position. Because Corning is growing, acquiring businesses and creating joint ventures, there are a lot of places for finance professionals to go and not a large number of candidates for each opening. If the company stopped growing, the situation would change.

Soft skills are being considered to an increasing degree in performance evaluations. Controller Dick Klein observes, "The higher you go, the more important the soft stuff becomes." Sometimes, managers suggest that people who need to develop those skills try to network with others who they believe have developed them very well.

Six years ago, the finance function published a list of behavioral characteristics (figure 8) to guide individuals and supervisors and to be used in the performance evaluation process.

FIGURE 8: Behaviors Valued by the Control and Finance Divisions

	INDIVIDUAL
Reliability/dependability	Doing what you said you would do.
Quality oriented	Applying the quality principles for reasons other than it being a corporate program.
Interpersonal skills	Acting in a way that people want to work with you. Able to work through conflict, neither avoiding it nor needlessly creating it.
Communications	Seeks opportunities to communicate, has an outward focus, and gathers appropriate information.
Team player	Is participative and values others' inputs and cooperation. Willing to cross organizational boundaries to accomplish team objectives.
Customer interaction	Provides appropriate customer output and maintains customer interface.
Credibility	Being perceived as believable, accurate, dependable, and responsible. Willing to be held accountable for one's own actions.
Reasoned thinking	Maintains a broad perspective or focus balanced with a sense of priority ("vital few"). Is viewed as common sensible and practical.
Creativity	Initiates new thinking and innovative ideas.
Flexibility	Able to react favorably to unusual workload or process changes, is adaptable to change.
Work ethic	Has a can-do/will-do attitude, willing to do what is needed and can deliver the goods under pressure.
	SUPERVISORY
Delegation	Appropriately uses human resources according to their abilities.
People development	Consistently looks to upgrading one's own and others' capabilities, skills, and contributions to the goals and objectives of the organization.

Corning's Diversity Initiatives: Finance Function a Leader

During the 1980s, the company recognized the direction demographics were moving in the United States and realized that minorities and women were underrepresented in its management ranks. CEO Houghton stated that the company's goal was to have a workforce that mirrors the national demographics "not only because it is right and moral but because it makes good business sense." Recruiting and retaining blacks and women was a particular challenge in a small town such as Corning in upstate New York. The company took special measures such as undergraduate internships, coaches for new minority employees, and even access to a black radio station and television station through the cable system. Gradually, those efforts are beginning to pay off. Between 1987 and 1993, women increased from 5 percent to 13 percent of the top 880 executives, and from 17 percent to 28 percent of total managers and professionals. In that time, blacks increased from 2 to 5 percent of the top 880 top executives and from 5 to 7 percent of total managers and professionals. Attrition was reduced from 16 percent per year in 1987 to 6.5 percent per year in 1993 for women, and from 15 percent to 10.5 percent for blacks.

Corning's efforts to promote diversity and help women and minorities break through the "glass ceiling" are well known. In the February 1992 issue of *Black Enterprise,* Corning was included on a list of 25 companies that exemplify the commitment and success potential of strong affirmative action programs. Corning was cited in a recent book by Lawrence Otis Graham, *The Best Companies for Minorities.* The company has made efforts to provide affordable housing in the Corning, New York, vicinity, to create opportunities for older workers, and to offer day care, leave, and other family benefits.

Controller Dick Klein explains that the finance function is expected to be a leader, way ahead of the corporate averages, because women have worked there for a long time. Klein's management staff is now about 47 percent women, the highest in the company. There is no problem finding women who are qualified to fill professional jobs at any level. Klein has three men and three women reporting to him as department heads. Minority goals have been tougher to achieve because there has been less of a universe to draw from.

Organization of the Finance Function

Financial functions at Corning are both centralized and decentralized. Some activities are accomplished more efficiently by one group for the entire corporation. Others lend themselves to a team approach and matrix reporting relationships.

The CFO, treasurer, and controller manage the overall financial structure of the corporation, including the debt/equity ratio. They oversee integrity, controls, and the movement of people in the finance function as a whole. Tax and treasury are largely centralized at the corporate level. Foreign subsidiaries have some autonomy, but the head office still sets the policy. Recruiting, personnel assignments, accounts receivable, and accounts payable are also centralized.

The finance function's approach to the centralization/decentralization issue is one of flexibility. A primary example of this flexibility is the treatment of the finance functions within Corning's wholly owned subsidiary, Corning Lab Services, Inc. In this case, Corning decided that several financial functions that are normally centralized were to be decentralized and to be responsive solely to Corning Lab Services, Inc., management. In this case, Corning's CFO felt that the function would achieve better results by being closer to and more responsible to the business.

Team Organization

Teams have a long history at Corning. A formal approach to teamwork began in 1987, when the company began to implement high-performance work systems in its plants. At that time, it established four quality principles: (1) meet customer requirements; (2) perform error-free work the first time and every time; (3) manage by prevention; and (4) measure by the cost of quality. It defined two types of customers, external and internal.

In the finance function at Corning, there are two types of teams. There are finance teams in each of the business units, and in the Administration Center, self-managed teams are responsible for many of the centralized financial functions.

Finance Teams in Business Units

Finance people work in teams in the business units at three levels: business teams, project teams, and strictly financial teams. Business teams comprise financial managers and people from other functions who work together and report to heads of business groups or divisions. Project teams have members from several functions who work together on specific tasks. For example, a finance person may work with engineering and production people on a new equipment investment proposal. Other teams work on processes that are strictly financial within the business units.

Most of the sector general managers, division general managers, and significant business managers have financial people as part of their business teams who help them reach decisions on strategy and work closely with them on almost all activities on a day-to-day basis. Rarely do financial people in the business units act just as consultants. For example, Alan Eusden, group financial manager for Specialty Materials, reports straight-line to the executive vice president for Specialty Materials and dotted-line to the senior vice president and controller. Although Eusden brings financial expertise to the team, he plays more than just a functional role. At his level, there is virtually no line between financial and general business discussions. He participates in every aspect of the team's thought and decision-making process, from pricing to marketing to costing.

As finance people gain experience in a business sector such as Specialty Materials, their job content gradually shifts from process work to projects and then to management and business strategy. Process work includes accounting entries, budgets, forecasts, purchase orders, inventory control, and payroll. It is typically supervised by the plant controller. Project work may include the analysis for an investment in new equipment. As people assume management responsibility, they become more involved in nonfinancial matters. Local strategy is concerned with what a specific smaller business unit is going to do over the next five years. Finance people interact with the commercial team. Global strategy is concerned with how an entire business area such as Specialty Materials is going to move, for example, in planned acquisitions and divestitures.

Figure 9 is an example of how job content changes with seniority for finance people in Specialty Materials. It shows an estimate of how time is allocated among various types of work for the five levels of finance people in the Specialty Materials Group.

FIGURE 9: How Financial People in Specialty Materials Allocate Their Time (percent)

	Process	*Team-based Projects*	*Management Team Interaction*	*Local Strategy*	*Global Strategy*
Assistant plant controller	50	30		20	
Plant controller	20	30	30	20	
Business controller	10	30	20	20	20
Division controller	10	30	30	10	20
Group financial manager	5	30	30		35

Although finance team members at each level spend about 30 percent of their time on team-based projects, the magnitude, complexity, visibility, and strategic impact of projects tend to be greater at a more senior level. An assistant plant controller may be doing a net present value analysis for a machine replacement; the group financial manager may be looking at the economic and political impacts of moving an operation from one country to another.

The people at the first two levels tend to be relatively new to the company. They work mostly on individual projects. At the more senior levels, people spend more of their time working with the higher level executives of the company. Management team interaction drops a little for business controllers and then moves up for division controllers and group financial managers. That is because business controllers tend to report to division controllers, whereas division controllers and group financial managers are members of senior managers' teams and are involved in a broader variety of business issues.

How a Team Improved the Closing Process

A financial team improved the closing process step by step using a method called IMPACT (Improvement Method for Process Analysis of Cost-Time). The team's objective was to reduce the cycle time, reduce errors, understand everything that could prevent a perfect closing, and by so doing, eliminate the need for a second closing. Van Campbell recalls, "We used to close about 10 or 11 on Thursday night after about 200 pizzas." On Friday morning, the data would be generated and analyzed and all the corrections would come in. Then there would be a second round leading to a final close on Saturday morning. Now the company closes by 4 p.m. on Thursday. The second closing is no longer required. What allowed this to happen, Campbell explains, is information sharing among teams throughout the company looking for ways to reduce errors and cycle time. Questions were asked such as, "What are we demanding from Corporate that makes it so difficult for them?" "What happens when the stuff flows in?" "Where do the errors come from?" There was recently an award for the closing team similar to the quality awards in the factories. This award gave recognition and a morale boost to a group of junior people who generate and process day-to-day work. It was a success story of bringing down barriers that keep people from working together.

Self-Managed Teams in Administration

The Administrative Center consists of 130 people who used to be part of five divisions. It is now a separate organization. Its responsibilities are managing benefit administration and a number of traditional finance functions that are centralized for the corporation. Benefit functions include pension administration, medical claims, workers' compensation, and disability. The finance functions include credit, payroll, accounts payable, and accounts receivable.

High-Performance Work Groups

The organization of the Administrative Center into "high-performance" self-managing work teams started in 1989. It was initiated by Van Campbell, vice chairman for Finance and Administration. At that time, treasury and control, including payroll and accounts payable, reported to him, but the benefit groups did not.

The objectives of the reorganization were to improve cost performance and customer service. Corning had had successful experiences with work teams and empowerment in a plant environment. This was the company's largest effort to develop the team concept in a staff organization.

In creating the Administrative Center, the company used consultants and renovated a building. In the words of Jack Simpson, co-manager of the center, it "redesigned how these people work together." All of the people came from within the company, but many of them had not worked together as part of the same organization.

Payroll Services Team

The Payroll Services Team has 15,000 customers in 38 states. Ruth Tucker organized a highly trained team of 10 and acts as business unit administrator and coach. The objectives of the team are as follows:

- Customer-focused business units
- Improved work environment
- Centralized leadership
- Improved decision making
- Improved technology
- Better coordination of services
- Lower costs
- Benefit from critical mass and synergy of resources

The team developed a skills matrix to help document the services provided and to decide on the number of people who should know each task. It developed a team hiring process, including selection criteria, and started to involve team members in the interviewing process. It developed a three- to five-year business plan, an annual high-performance plan, and a plan for transition to a truly self-managed team.

The team received both technical training and soft-skills training. The soft-skills training included team effectiveness, giving and receiving constructive feedback, managing meetings, valuing diversity, running meetings, and other team-building skills.

Credit and Collection

Formerly, the credit and accounts receivable functions were separated. People doing cash applications were not part of the same function as credit. Credit people didn't like receivables people talking to the customer. Today, they sit together as part of the same work teams. They are cross-trained, subject to control constraints such as separation of duties. Credit people will now do cash applications if they have extra time or if there is an absence.

Export Billing

Corning has both a domestic and international credit function. International credit and international invoicing for the whole company are now the responsibility of one team in the Administrative Center. Business units send data to the Administrative Center, which prepares export invoices for shipments.

Accounts Payable

In the past, individual people were assigned to individual functions such as data entry, calculation of cash discount, and checking for systems authorization. Now everyone does the whole function. People's responsibilities are separated alphabetically by vendor. This provides the vendor with one person to talk to on the telephone. A person who processes the invoice from start to finish can answer all of a customer's questions. Before, vendor inquiry people got all the questions, but they couldn't answer them without having to go to other desks or to the files. Before, it was considered efficient for a keypunch operator to specialize, pick up speed, and keypunch all day. But that person did not know anything about other jobs such as vendor coding. If the vendor coding person got sick, there was a problem. Today, the absent person's invoices would be merged with someone else's. Jack Simpson reports, "They all know how to do the whole function."

Team Organization and Supervision

Originally, there were seven people per supervisor. Now there are 15. That happened partly through attrition and partly through teams becoming self-managed. Teams are assuming more responsibility for dealing with customers, both external and internal. Supervisors and managers are encouraged to become coaches and leaders, establishing direction, coordinating training, and making sure that teams have the right tools.

Teams schedule their own work hours and take advantage of flextime. The team as a whole might adhere to a guideline such as covering the phones from 7 a.m. to 6 p.m. for customer calls. Because of the team approach, coverage has increased. Teams schedule vacations, make sure jobs are covered, and arrange for personal time to be made up. Supervisors do not sign time cards.

Training

Training is about 5 percent of the individual's work year. It includes social skills such as dealing with feedback, conflict resolution, customer service, how to answer the phones, and how to deal with an angry customer. Social skills learning is tougher than other professional and technical training.

Teams do a lot of cross-training. A system of skill-based pay, encouraging team members to learn more functions, is being developed with the help of consultants.

Team Performance Targets

Every year, the High-Performance Plan includes goals and functional objectives that teams use to measure themselves and review with supervisors and managers. Specific performance targets may include days sales outstanding, percent of receivables current, and spending compared to budget. Other more qualitative objectives may include supervisors' responsibilities that should be assumed by teams or customer-related decisions that should be made by credit correspondents.

Figure 10 shows the goals and objectives of the Administrative Center, and figure 11 shows the guiding principles. Figure 12 shows the criteria by which teams rate their own performance, and figure 13 shows the criteria by which teams evaluate how well the Administrative Center measures up to its own vision.

FIGURE 10: Administrative Center Goals and Objectives

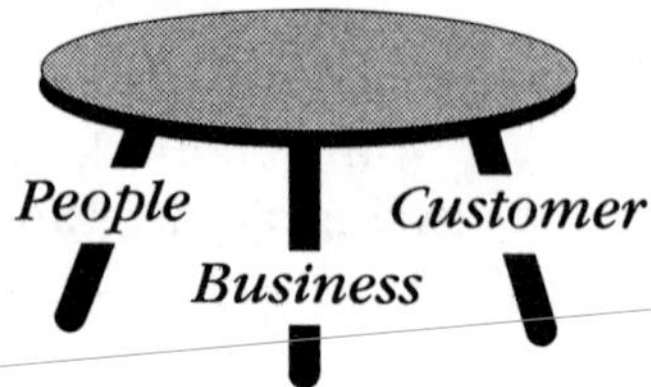

People

Support a high-performance environment where employees are empowered, skilled, and motivated to achieve their full potential.

Business

Provide services in a competitive, financially sound manner exceeding profitability targets.

Customer

Provide exceptional service through proactive customer partnerships.

FIGURE 11: Administrative Center Guiding Principles

Mission

SERVICE! SERVICE! SERVICE!

Vision

Empowered people delighting customers

Values

- ☐ People working together
- ☐ Customer focus
- ☐ Business-driven technology

Guiding Principles

In pursuit of our mission, we will

- ☐ Excel in delivering customer-focused services
- ☐ Encourage a creative, innovative, and challenging work environment
- ☐ Fully utilize the quality principles
- ☐ Require the involvement and commitment of every team member
- ☐ Encourage people to make decisions, take action, and be responsible for the outcomes of those actions
- ☐ Treat every individual with respect and dignity, and value diversity as a source of strength

- ☐ Ensure an environment where communication is open and information is shared
- ☐ Recognize and reward performance, knowledge, skills, and contributions
- ☐ Provide training to meet our goals
- ☐ Celebrate success

FIGURE 12: High-Performance Criteria Rating for Business Units

(Each factor is graded on a scale of 1 to 7.

1 = Disagree; 4 = Somewhat agree; 7 = Agree)

A. Physical Proximity of Business Units

1. Team members are in frequent daily contact with each other.

B. High-Performance Plan/Day-to-Day Operations

1. High-performance plans are incorporated into day-to-day operations, reviewed and updated on a quarterly basis.
2. The team continuously challenges traditional approaches to getting the job done.
3. The team takes responsibility and ownership for the business processes and outputs.
4. The team has identified and mapped key processes and is currently making progress using IMPACT.
5. The team has a documentation plan in place and is currently making progress on the plan.
6. The team's skills matrix is being used to develop cross-training plans and documentation needs.
7. Appropriate resources to perform day-to-day operations are made available to the team.
8. Necessary information is made available to all team members.
9. Teams measure and display KRIs.
10. I have a clear understanding of the goal-sharing plan measures and how they affect the overall performance.

C. Social Skills

1. Meetings are efficient and results oriented.
2. All team members participate in meeting discussions.
3. Decisions are made by consensus.
4. Team members have a tolerance for conflict with an emphasis on growth, learning, and resolution.
5. When the team discusses problems, the emphasis is on shared responsibility for improvement rather than blaming.
6. The team uses problem-solving skills such as brainstorming, defining the problem, analyzing data, etc.
7. Team members do an effective job of listening to each other.
8. There is a balance of dealing with problems and recognizing successes.
9. I have a career plan in place.

FIGURE 12: High-Performance Criteria Rating for Business Units (continued)

D. Business Skills

1. Team members are increasing their knowledge of the team budget.
2. The team has a plan in place to survey and/or get feedback from their customers (focus groups, mail surveys, phone surveys, etc.).
3. Team members know and understand their customers' requirements and expectations and are attempting to meet or exceed them.
4. All team members have the skills necessary to meet day-to-day business needs.
5. Team members place a high emphasis on customer service and continue to seek training to improve.
6. Team goals and objectives are understood by all team members.
7. All team members are involved in setting business goals and objectives.
8. Team members are aware of, and involved in, the development of their business plan.

FIGURE 13: Administrative Center Vision Rating

(Rating scale 1 = Never; 2 = Rarely; 3 = Sometimes; 4 = Most of the Time; 5 = Always)

Category	*Rating*	*Category*	*Rating*
Trust		Appropriate technology for business needs	
Change		People want to join organization	
Energy		Value added	
Self-starting people		Known and respected as leading high-performance work system	
Ownership		Celebrating success	
Proud to work here		Supplier of choice	
Involvement		Customers say "WOW"	
Commitment		Support	
People feel like winners		Ideas are welcomed	
Respect		Training	
People feel rewarded/proud		Information shared	
"Can-do" attitude		Career development opportunities	
Decision making		Continuous process improvement	
Fun		Baldrige/quality	
Open communication		Diversity	
Team effort			
People growth and development			
Great work environment			
Exceptional customer service			

6

W. L. Gore and Associates, Inc.

Interview Subject: *Shanti Mehta, Associate*

Executive Summary

At W. L. Gore and Associates, a distinctive corporate culture was established at the outset. From the time of its founding in 1958, the company has had a team organization that completely takes the place of a more traditional hierarchy. Founder Wilbert L. Gore created an informal atmosphere and established what became known as a lattice organizational structure as a reaction to the large corporate bureaucratic environment in which he had spent his career before founding his own company.

In Gore's lattice organizational structure, there are no titles and no one reports to anyone else. A finance person joining the company must find a way to be useful and persuade a team that he or she can make a useful contribution. How peers judge a person's contribution is the basis of pay; longevity is not a factor. Initiatives such as planning and forecasting systems and business decision reports bubble up from finance people on teams throughout the company. Useful ideas are adopted by other business units. Gore has no formal capital budgeting process. A product champion assembles an advisory group, which helps the champion decide whether or not to go ahead with a project and provides advice in periodic opportunity review meetings. The associates at Gore believe that empowering each person and allowing each person to make the contribution for which his or her talents are best suited not only unleashes creativity but also makes the company comparatively efficient. The cost of the finance function as a percentage of sales is lower here than in most large companies. There is only one person in the head-office treasury function.

Background

The company is best known as the maker of GoreTex® fabric, which is used for outdoor gear, artificial arteries and ligaments, air and water filters, and even dental floss. Sales have grown about 20 percent annually in the past decade and are now over $800 million. Approximately 5,700 employees work in 50 plants worldwide.

As a highly regarded research chemist at DuPont, Bill Gore had been part of a task force experimenting with applications for polytetrafluoroethylene, known as PTFE, or Teflon™. Gore conducted experiments in his home basement laboratory with the help of his son Bob, and discovered that PTFE could be used to insulate ribbon cable wires. He thought that PTFE would have ideal insulating characteristics for transistors and computers. However, he was unable to interest the company in his new product ideas. DuPont preferred to be a raw material supplier rather than a fabricator. Against the advice of his more risk-averse friends, Bill Gore and his wife Vieve mortgaged their house and drew on savings to found a new company. As with most new businesses, cash was tight in the first few years. Some employees accepted board in the Gores' house in lieu of part of their salaries.

Bill Gore died in 1986 pursuing his favorite pastime of mountain hiking. Today, his son Bob is president of the company and his wife Vieve is the corporate secretary. Aside from those two legally required titles, and the occasional designation of Shanti Mehta as chief financial officer, there are no titles in the company.

Guiding Principles and Core Values

From the beginning, W. L. Gore has had an informal style and has strived to minimize bureaucracy and overhead. Looking back on 28 years in a large organization, Bill Gore observed that thick layers of management could stifle creativity. As his own company grew, he wanted to maintain the original camaraderie and entrepreneurial spirit.

It is the company's policy for no more than 200 employees to work in one plant. This stemmed from Gore's realization at one point that the original Newark, Delaware, plant had grown too large for him to know everyone on a first-name basis.

Bill Gore asked his associates to follow four principles:

- **Fairness:** Each of us will *try* to be fair in all dealings—with each other, with our suppliers, with our customers, within our communities, and with all people with whom we have transactions or agreements. Fairness is seldom clearly defined, but if a sincere effort is made by all, it generates a tolerance that preserves good feelings among us.
- **Freedom:** Each of us will allow, help, and encourage his Associates to grow in knowledge, skill, the scope of responsibility, and the range of activities. Authority is gained by recognized knowledge or skill. It is not a power of command, only of leadership.
- **Commitment:** Each of us will make his own commitments—and keep them. No Associate can impose a commitment on another. All commitments are self-commitments.

  We organize our Enterprise—projects, functions, and work of all kinds—through commitments. Therefore, a commitment is a serious matter, amounting to a contract that must be fulfilled.
- **Waterline:** Each of us will consult with appropriate Associates who will share the responsibility of taking any action that has the potential of serious harm to the reputation, success, or survival of the Enterprise.

  The analogy is that our Enterprise is like a ship that we are all in together. Boring holes above the waterline is not serious, but below the waterline, holes could sink our ship.

Shanti Mehta recalls other values articulated by Gore that remain a foundation of the company culture to this day and particularly affect the philosophy of the finance function. Gore's values were to make money and have fun; to concentrate on cash flow, not profits; and to avoid financial leverage. Gore said that profits were for accountants to pay taxes, but it was cash flow that really mattered. He did not care if debt was cheaper than equity because debt could cause difficulty in bad economic times. The company's only debt is relatively inexpensive industrial revenue bonds, and its leverage is less than 10 percent. W. L. Gore's prices are never based on cost, but on the value of the product. If the value of the product is less than the cost, the company figures out how to enhance the value or reduce the cost, but value is always the driver.

The Lattice Organization

The most distinctive feature of the culture at W. L. Gore is the lattice organization. It stems from Bill Gore's observation that in every successful organization there is an underground lattice that disseminates information and gets things done. At W. L. Gore, there is no hierarchy; no one reports to anyone. Mehta says, "I report to my conscience and my commitment and so does every other associate in the company." Everyone can have a direct line of communication with everyone else. There are no titles and no job descriptions. Everyone is called an associate; the term "employee" is not used. Associates have sponsors but not bosses. Tasks and objectives are not assigned by managers; they are defined by personal commitments and cooperative team efforts.

How Teams Are Formed

Self-directed teams are the essence of the company's organization. The company as a whole is a big empowered team; each plant is a team; there are countless teams organized by function and task. Most of them are not formally designated; they tend to be self-developing and fluid, constantly forming and disbanding.

Financial Teams

W. L. Gore has no centralized accounting and financial function, though it does have centralized reports. The finance function is decentralized. Local financial teams support both plants and business units that are formed around products. Rather than being part of a companywide finance function structure, the teams are responsible only to the businesses and plants where they are located. Sponsorship for accounting and financial functions lies squarely with the business leaders in those areas. If a product is made in more than one plant, product and plant financial team functions may overlap.

Team Leadership

Bill Gore said, "We don't appoint leaders; leaders have followers." In the financial and accounting teams, leaders are not appointed; they emerge out of groups working together.

Recruiting Finance Professionals

Most of W. L. Gore's hiring is for scientists and engineers. Because the company has a relatively lean finance function and little turnover, new finance people are not hired very often. In the company's Newark, Delaware, headquarters and cluster of 15 plants nearby, only two finance people have been hired in the past eight years.

An individual may send in a resume after finding out about W. L. Gore through an article in a business magazine, through mention in other publications such as Robert Levering and Milton Moskowitz's book *100 Best Companies to Work for in America,* or through word of mouth. The Human Resources Department receives all resumes, as well as requests from within the company for finance people with certain backgrounds and skills.

After receiving and reviewing a resume, a human resources associate may call around to see if there is any interest, and if there is, invite the candidate for an interview. It is a policy that at least five associates who have been with the company five years or more interview each candidate. A candidate who is a finance professional is interviewed by business leaders; associates from different functions such as human resources, engineering, and research; and at least one financial person. Unanimous agreement among the interviewers is required for a job offer to be made.

The rigor is the same for every candidate, though the level of people who do the interviewing may vary. For example, the company may need a receivables clerk with a high school diploma and some accounting background. If no interest in the position is expressed internally, an advertisement is placed in a local newspaper. After passing an initial screening by human resources, the candidate is interviewed by five people who judge qualities such as the capability to work as part of a team. Mehta says, "We don't want individualists who function just for themselves, but people who have team working ability and good interpersonal skills; pleasant people who are also technically competent."

Role of the Sponsor

From the earliest days of the company, Bill Gore was concerned about helping new people get started and following their progress. Since then, it has been a company policy that before a person is hired, an associate must agree to act as that person's sponsor. The sponsor is usually part of the interviewing process, and takes a keen interest in a person's initial acceptance in the organization. In Mehta's words, the sponsor acts as a "friend, philosopher, and guide," being available when the new associate needs someone to talk to, and being able to address problems of any kind.

In the beginning, the associate needs to know where the stockroom is, where to get pencils and paper, whom to call for various other needs. The sponsor may meet the person every day if they work in the same area, or perhaps every week if they are more distant. The sponsor's objective is to help the associate to become successful, growing both intellectually, by way of contribution, and materially, in terms of compensation. This is a mentoring process in which the new associate is taken under the sponsor's wing for a year or two; there is no command structure, and the sponsor is not a boss. An associate can reject a sponsor and request a different one. The initial sponsor is not expected to object. But each person will always have a sponsor, and most associates become sponsors after they have been with the company some time.

Finding a Place and Making a Commitment

There are no assigned jobs at W. L. Gore. It is up to the individual to find a place. A new associate may recommend how he or she could make a contribution based on recognized needs, individual interests, or prior experience. A team may indicate a need or respond to an individual's suggestion. Rather than being directed by the company or a boss to do something, the individual makes a commitment.

An associate may have a background in finance through schooling, practical experience, or both. Opportunities to work in a financial capacity may have been discussed during the recruiting process. The individual may have expressed interest in certain functions such as general ledger, preparing financial reports, foreign exchange exposure management, or banking relationships. After coming on board, the person would be expected to use those ideas and interests as a basis for getting to know other associates involved with finance, what various teams are doing, and where their needs are.

Finding out what needs to be done, making proposals on new tasks that have not been done in the past, and joining teams are processes of negotiation. The actual content of the job depends in large part on individual initiative. A person might say, "I don't want to have a bookkeeping role in the accounting group; I want to do financial analysis on a broader scale." The individual sells a team, business unit, or plant on the business benefits of a new type of financial analysis, and in that process negotiates a place to fit in. Upon joining a team, the individual is not assigned a task or function, but rather makes a personal commitment to the team.

Finance Career Paths

Associates may enlarge their responsibilities and find new assignments through a combination of initiative and networking. A person may develop and perform a function in a plant or business unit that is not being performed elsewhere in the company. Word of the individual's talents gets around.

There is room for people who want to be just finance specialists, and there is room for people who want to use their financial skills while evolving into a broader management role. Sometimes a financial person discovers the challenges of business management to be more interesting than acting in a more specialized technical or functional capacity. One analyst who was interested in pricing decisions became involved with a product for which pricing was an important part of the competitive strategy. To develop the pricing strategy, he needed to become involved in every aspect of the business and eventually become the business leader for the product.

Self-Initiated Team Efforts in Finance

A team of four associates in Flagstaff, Arizona, is responsible for business planning and forecasting for the company's entire medical group. They developed a reputation for reliable forecasting and business plans that made sense and held up over time. Their reports showed how the business was doing compared to plan on a worldwide basis, providing sufficient but not excessive detail. Mehta recognized what they were doing and asked them to make a presentation in Delaware to give ideas to other business units.

A two-person team became interested in fixed-assets management at a local level, noticing that some of the accounting procedures were sloppy and that some fixed assets should have been written off but were still on the books. Based on their guidelines, fixed-asset accounting was reviewed in all of the company's plants.

A team with a manufacturing background became interested in inventory management and took courses on world-class manufacturing. Team members discovered that raw material and finished-goods inventory were generally not a problem, but that there were opportunities to reduce work-in-process inventory and to reduce lead times accordingly. The team is now applying world-class manufacturing principles to the entire organization.

Two associates working in Germany and England have cooperated to produce business decision reports that depart significantly from accounting reports, and particularly from reports prepared for tax purposes. When materials are sent from the United States to foreign plants, IRS regulations require transfer pricing to be at arm's length and to include U.S. manufacturing overhead and profits. Such a price is much higher than what W. L. Gore considers to be its real cost, and therefore causes the foreign plants to report what are considered to be artificially low profits. That is fine for tax purposes but not for business planning and performance evaluation. The team that developed the business decision reports is spending some time in the United States helping the company apply its system worldwide.

The company's data processing activities are closely tied with the finance function. A computer scientist with a financial background helped to create an ordering system to alleviate a telephone bottleneck when the company introduced a new Gore-Tex dental floss product called Glide. Because a nationwide distribution system had not been developed for the new product, about 6,000 calls each month for relatively small orders came directly to company headquarters. In one week, a team of two data processing associates put together a PC-based system with three telephone operators. A customer could tell the operator his or her ZIP Code and receive the name of the nearest store to buy the product, or could use a credit card and have the order shipped the same day.

Role of the Product Champion in Capital Budgeting

W. L. Gore does not use capital budgeting procedures such as internal rate of return and net present value. The company is more concerned with the process of screening the innumerable product ideas that emerge, deciding which ones to work on, and trying to avoid putting money and associates' time into projects that will fail. Many of the product ideas that are approved start as single-person projects. As the project progresses, the person must assume the role of product champion, deciding when to ask other associates to join in and build a team. At various stages, the product champion asks a group of colleagues he or she respects to join in an opportunity review meeting. The champion might review the original idea, demonstrate the prototype product, describe what it will do, why it is unique, or how it compares to similar products made by other companies, and ask for a sum, say a million dollars, to begin production. The opportunity group asks questions and decides whether to appropriate the funds required. The group meets often enough to help the product champion decide quickly to drop a project that is not working out before additional resources are wasted.

People have started projects that looked very promising in the beginning, spent as much as $20 to $25 million, and built teams as large as 100 people. Suddenly, they have discovered that what was planned could not be done. If the whole process is approached the right way, the decision to stop is accepted. The product champion is recognized for having tried, and mistakes are tolerated. What counts is the way the product champion goes about starting the project and consulting peers. When the outlook for a project turns sour, it is equally important for the product champion to have the courage to bring people together and make a decision to terminate it quickly.

Ongoing Performance Evaluation

Performance evaluation is a continuous, year-round process. An associate's noteworthy achievements are publicized within the company and celebrated immediately. Special meetings are called. Awards are given. Keeping the performance appraisal process going on a daily and weekly basis is one of a sponsor's important responsibilities. When some aspect of performance is perceived as not being up to the company's standards, say not getting a job done when planned or damaging a working relationship with another associate, it is the sponsor's duty to take the associate aside and discuss the problem frankly. By the time the company's more formal six-month and annual reviews take place, an associate usually has an idea of how well his or her performance is being perceived.

Playing on Individual Strengths

It is W. L. Gore's philosophy to allow people to use their strengths to the maximum. To the extent possible, their weaknesses should be minimized, or just ignored. This allows people with highly individual creative talents to concentrate where they believe they can make the most effective contribution, and not be fettered by other duties that are lower priorities and that do not capitalize on their strengths.

Compensation Based on Contribution

The company is more concerned with an individual's contribution than in performance evaluation per se. Individuals are paid based on their contributions to the financial success of the enterprise, not on the number of years they have spent with the company. Contribution is the focal point of an elaborate compensation system the company is very proud of. The system is administered by compensation committees consisting of specialists in functions such as accounting and finance and knowledgeable business leaders. The committees meet every six months. Individual associates judge and rank fellow associates, and business leaders make similar judgments and rankings.

There may be 50 associates in an area such as accounting and finance. They are ranked starting with the person who has made the highest contribution, the second highest, the third highest, and on to the lowest. Presumably, each associate in an area such as finance has a reasonable idea of what other finance associates are doing, whether they are whiling away their time, talking all the time, or really accomplishing something solid such as increasing productivity. Each associate ranks all the other associates based on his or her own judgment and definition of contribution. The peer group rankings are consolidated into one list. Then a similar list is created by business leaders working in the same plant. Associates suggest others outside the immediate area who may have some useful input, such as people in nonfinancial functions. Other advocates in the company, such as a receptionist or a plant associate, may comment on attitude and demeanor.

All of these lists are pulled together. A computer program is used to average and weight the rankings and plot the consolidated rankings on a chart. On the X axis, associates are ranked by contribution from 1 to 50. The Y axis is used to correlate company salaries with salaries for comparable jobs in the region. It is left blank in the beginning and filled in as individual contributions are matched with benchmark jobs and salaries in nearby companies.

The committee may look at what the person ranked number one in finance is doing—for example, looking after accounting for the whole corporation or serving as a plant controller. The committee considers what similar people are paid elsewhere. A plant controller may be paid more than counterparts in other companies; the committee discusses why. He may be considered more valuable than the normal plant controller because he has a variety of other responsibilities and skills. Another person may be a good bookkeeper and capable of preparing financial statements, but not very good at interpreting them. He has a bachelor's degree in accounting but appears not to have developed very much. Compensation levels are plotted on the chart based on external benchmarks for all these individuals, and a line is drawn from the highest paid to the lowest paid.

Inevitably there are valleys and peaks, and the committee has to ask why the second ranked or the twentieth ranked associate is being paid more or less than the line would indicate. People around the table debate the pros and cons of various associates and question their ranking. The ranking may be considered unfair for a person because of bad input. For instance, one person may dislike another person and give a poor ranking. A consensus emerges, from which the committee decides how to adjust each person's compensation.

Some bright individuals have doubled their compensation during their first year with the company. This requires not only good performance but visibility. The associate must take the initiative to make his or her contribution visible in ways such as keeping the sponsor informed, writing articles, giving presentations, teaching seminars, and helping others. In this way, the individual develops a span of influence throughout the organization. When highly successful associates have been in the company for five or ten years, their contributions become well known and the compensation committee needs less formal feedback from other associates.

Not everyone chooses the fast track, nor are they required to. This is recognized and accepted in the compensation system. Some associates have not received salary raises other than cost-of-living adjustments for as long as 10 years. They have chosen more static jobs, preferring to work in a low-pressure, nine-to-five environment.

The compensation committee goes through the full exercise once a year, and then gives the results a six-month interim review for any important changes in individuals' contributions. In all, the compensation review process takes about three weeks per year of each senior business leader's time.

No associate better demonstrates the process of coming on board and finding a way to make a contribution than does Gore's Shanti Mehta. He studied physics as an undergraduate and statistics at the graduate level. In his early years with the company, he worked in the research and development function. During the 1974 recession, Bill Gore, then chairman, said that the company did not have anyone who really understood numbers, uncertainty, and probabilities. He wanted to have a better idea of which products were making money and which were not. He asked Mehta to get involved in the finance function and do an analysis to show profitability by product line. Despite Mehta's caveat that he had never attended a finance or accounting class, Gore expressed confidence that he could do it and asked for his commitment. Mehta liked his new responsibilities and found that many of the disciplines he had learned in mathematics and statistics, and even in physics, were applicable to the finance function.

Mehta developed his own approaches to cost and profitability analysis, free from any conceptual constraints he might have had if he had been trained on the accounting side of the business. For example, Mehta points out that under the name of cost accounting, huge bureaucracies can be set up to calculate standard costs. He does not believe in calculating unit costs and thinks that overhead allocation tends to be nonsense. W. L. Gore does not use cost as a basis for pricing. Nonetheless, Mehta admits that the company still has to estimate the costs for its various products. The company has a good idea of fixed and variable costs and focuses on the variable cost that is absorbed for each product. Statistical sampling is often used for estimating variable costs, and regression analysis can be helpful in estimating fixed and variable costs. Mehta found that his mathematical background helped him think independently about the allocation of capital among W. L. Gore's products, appropriate financial measurement criteria, and valuation of the company.

Though W. L. Gore is privately held, it must continually have an up-to-date valuation to determine the stock transfer price for its employee stock ownership plan, which it calls an associate stock ownership plan (ASOP). The company uses outside consultants to help determine a fair market value as if it were publicly traded.

As Mehta continually emphasizes, the company has no levels. He considers himself a resource who can be valuable because of his experience, 25 years with the company, and knowledge of all the company's businesses. Mehta recognizes that he is not skilled in some financial areas, and he refers questions in areas such as depreciation and other aspects of accounting to specialists.

Financial Information Sharing

Shanti Mehta uses his experience to help business leaders assemble the information they need to be successful, and he also acts as a watchdog on a worldwide basis. By keeping abreast of what is happening in each country and continually scanning and comparing various units' monthly reports, he can often spot anomalies and trends that individual plant leaders and product managers might overlook.

One of Mehta's proudest accomplishments has been working with other associates to develop a worldwide management information system. Their challenge was to develop a system that was appropriate for a multinational company with 50 plants, provided an overview, allowed "peeling the onion," and provided the detailed information that the user might want, but that did not produce unnecessarily long reports.

By the third or fourth working day of every month, the company is able to print out general ledgers and detailed financial reports for its 32 U.S. plants and business units. By the tenth working day, reports are available from all units, worldwide. They are compiled in a centralized worldwide information system in the company's head office in Newark, Delaware. The reports can be accessed at any location in the United States through the company's network. They can be viewed by Mehta or by associates in other plants for benchmarking purposes. Business leaders overseas see worldwide reports quarterly. Often they are scientists and marketers who are preoccupied with their own concerns and do not spend very much time analyzing financial performance reports. They can benefit from having exceptions in their business-unit reports pointed out to them in an occasional phone call from Mehta. In a similar way, Mehta keeps CEO Bob Gore, who is primarily a scientist, abreast of financial information he needs to know.

By the tenth to twelfth working day of every month, Mehta prepares a five-minute financial bulletin on cassette tape to explain the company's financial performance for the year to date. It is sent to every unit through the company's worldwide voice mail system and heard by every associate in the company, including the CEO, members of the board, business leaders, sales people, research scientists, engineers, and production workers.

How the Lattice Organization Creates Efficiency

Mehta cites a recent article published in the *Wall Street Journal* in which a consultant estimated that the financial function costs 1.5 percent of sales in a typical centralized company and 2.5 percent in a decentralized company, and that the finance staff generally represents 10 to 15 percent of salaried personnel in nonfinancial companies. W. L. Gore's finance function costs are less than 1 percent of sales. Mehta considers this to be a direct result of the company's philosophy of doing what is necessary, eliminating non-value-added activities, and allowing people to create their own jobs and manage their own priorities. This is illustrated by the company's one-person treasury function and the way it manages its financial institution relationships.

The Cash Manager

W. L. Gore's entire treasury function is the responsibility of one certified cash manager working with Mehta. Her responsibilities include cash management, cash flow projections, short-term investments, foreign exchange exposure management, and banking relationships. She uses a treasury workstation, does reconciliation for banking accounts, and checks to see that all interest calculations for short-term investments are correct. She and Mehta manage foreign exchange exposure together and retain a team from Brown Brothers Harriman, the New York private banking firm, as consultants. Mehta says, "We have empowered her, trusted her, and given her the freedom to grow." She is a high school graduate who developed an interest in accounting while she was a production worker. She convinced Mehta that she had an aptitude for cash management and received tuition assistance to take courses at a nearby university. She became a certified cash manager the first time she took the examination. In contrast, Mehta points to nearby chemical companies where 30 or 40 people report to an assistant treasurer. He reiterates, "The reason we can operate that way is empowerment. We do not believe in titles, structure. We have no hierarchy."

Financial Institution Relationships

A number of years ago, Mehta and his associates decided that they wanted to do business with only the best financial institutions in the country. For commercial banks, they picked J. P. Morgan and Wachovia for reasons including their top credit ratings and reputations for service quality; Bank of Delaware, now part of PNC Corporation, as their local bank; and Brown Brothers Harriman as "a private bank with conservative traditions." They picked Goldman Sachs because it was universally considered to be one of the top investment banking firms. Mehta explains that the company does business with these firms and no others. These bankers understand W. L. Gore and its structure. They know not to make unnecessary social visits just to maintain contact. They know not to ask W. L. Gore people out to lunch, but that if they wish they may bring sandwiches and talk in the conference room. Mehta says, "Once every three or four months is fine. If there is something special, we can talk about it. Otherwise, we do not have to waste time at lunches, dinners, and meetings."

Reconciling Control and Empowerment

The company is not particularly concerned about the internal control standards of generally accepted accounting principles (GAAP) and as a result is sometimes criticized by auditors. A person might have too many functions, such as signing checks and doing reconciliations. Mehta answers such criticism by explaining that this is the company's style. "People write checks, get signatures, and they are sent. We have never had a problem, and if there is, we think we can stand it. After one minor incident, a person was fired and that was the end of it. We do not want to sacrifice the principle of trust. We delegate responsibility and empower a person, and the person is responsible to his or her conscience. This philosophy has worked for more than 30 years."

Why People Leave the Company

The unstructured environment without titles, job definitions, and directions from the boss is not for everyone. Some people join the company and then have a hard time finding a niche, perhaps because they are used to being directed, because they are shy in introducing themselves to people and negotiating a place to fit in, or because they do not have enough initiative. Some have poor interpersonal skills even though they are technically qualified. Some are uncomfortable in a team setting. Though firing for cause is sometimes necessary, people generally make their own decision to leave because they are frustrated at not being able to find a place where they can contribute and be recognized.

Where the Lattice Structure Is Best Applied

Bill Gore believed that the lattice organizational structure could work only if established by an entrepreneur in a start-up company. He thought that it would be difficult to create such a structure in an organization with an established hierarchy. For a research-driven company such as W. L. Gore and Associates, and for individuals willing to adapt and make the commitment, it appears to work very well.

7

Harley-Davidson, Inc.

Interview Subjects: *Richard F. Teerlink, president and chief executive officer; James Ziemer, vice president and chief financial officer; James Brostowitz, vice president and controller; John A. Hevey, director of finance, Marketing Operations*

Executive Summary

Harley-Davidson is one of the best examples of an American industrial company that has been able to restore its competitiveness after a period of difficulty. Cultural change has been an essential element in the company's financial turnaround. One of the principal leaders of that change has been Rich Teerlink, formerly CFO and now CEO. To build internal partnerships and improve information flow among the company's various functions, Harley-Davidson has flattened its organizational structure into three intersecting circles: marketing, manufacturing, and support. Functions such as finance are represented in each circle. Through a process known as fence setting, groups and individuals negotiate, define, and adjust their responsibilities.

Harley-Davidson's planning is a process of forcing down and forcing up. Top management first defines goals without dollar figures, which are in effect forced down into the business units. More specific plans including sales targets and budgets are forced back up for approval. Finance people act as advocates rather than naysayers in the approval process. Teerlink believes that the major task of the finance function is to help people understand what value-added activities are. To do that, finance people need to get out of finance and work in other areas for parts of their careers to understand the real world. Teerlink believes that the first issue of quality for the finance function is to understand who its customers are, and that the most important customers are not the outside world or top management, but people inside the organization who are preparing budgets and incurring costs.

Background

Harley-Davidson was founded in 1903 at the dawn of the motorcycle industry. It became the leader at the heavy end of the market, and the name became a legend. The image of the motorcycle rider with the black leather jacket was the Harley-Davidson image. Although the brand never lost its core following of loyal customers and employees, the company went through tough times in the 1970s and 1980s and nearly failed. Japanese motorcycles penetrated the lighter market and started to attack the heavy end. Harley-Davidson was acquired by AMF and run by the numbers as just one more business in a large conglomerate. In 1981, as many conglomerates were shedding subsidiaries, Harley-Davidson was taken private in an LBO. Through the leadership of Vaughn Beals, former Motorcycle Group executive with AMF, the company had, at last, the freedom to reinvent itself, but still faced a crushing debt burden that threatened its survival.

During this emergency period, the finance function played a crucial role in Harley-Davidson's survival. Cash flow was paramount. Almost all decisions were finance decisions. More than one-quarter of the workforce was let go. Even sales strategies were oriented toward getting rid of inventory to raise cash. The finance function established a systems framework to ensure that cash flow was an important element in most decisions.

Richard Teerlink joined the company as CFO in 1981, two months after the buy-out. He became president and chief operating officer in 1987 and CEO in 1989. Under his leadership, the company began to grapple with what it was and what it stood for. What continued to inspire the loyal core of customers and employees was more than a product; it was also an image and a lifestyle. These intangibles were the foundation on which Beals and the management team defined who the stakeholders were, and the values and vision that would allow the company to survive and prosper.

The marketing group embarked on a campaign to reestablish the brand name. Promotion was centered on a theme of "close to the customer." The Harley Owners Group (HOG) was established and has grown to 220,000 members worldwide, more than 40 percent of the company's customer base.

The Business Process

Reviving the company required getting everyone involved. Teerlink points to the company's Business Process Flow Chart, explaining, "We run the business through process; there's a whole lot that goes on, and it all connects." The Business Process Flow Chart shows how the company's values and vision affect all corporate stakeholders, including the company's employees. (See figure 14.) It starts with an umbrella, which is the corporate vision. "Our vision is simple," says Teerlink, "continuous improvement activities to continuously improve the quality of profitable relationships with all of our stakeholders. That's what we are in business to do." The chart shows that the vision is influenced by the company's basic values, the current business issues it considers most important, and the interests of all the company's stakeholders, which must be balanced.

The vision is a foundation for the Business Process, or what Teerlink describes as the 150-year plan (figure 15). It provides a framework for each of the operating divisions to decide their missions, operating philosophies, and objectives. That in turn provides each work unit within a division the basis for the function strategy and work unit plans for each area, and for individual career and performance plans. Then, in the annual planning cycle, everything gets forced back up. This is an essential part of the process. Teerlink says that nonleadership people are participating more than leadership people in the forcing-up process, and that this will require the behavior of the company's leaders to change.

FIGURE 14: Business Process Flow Chart

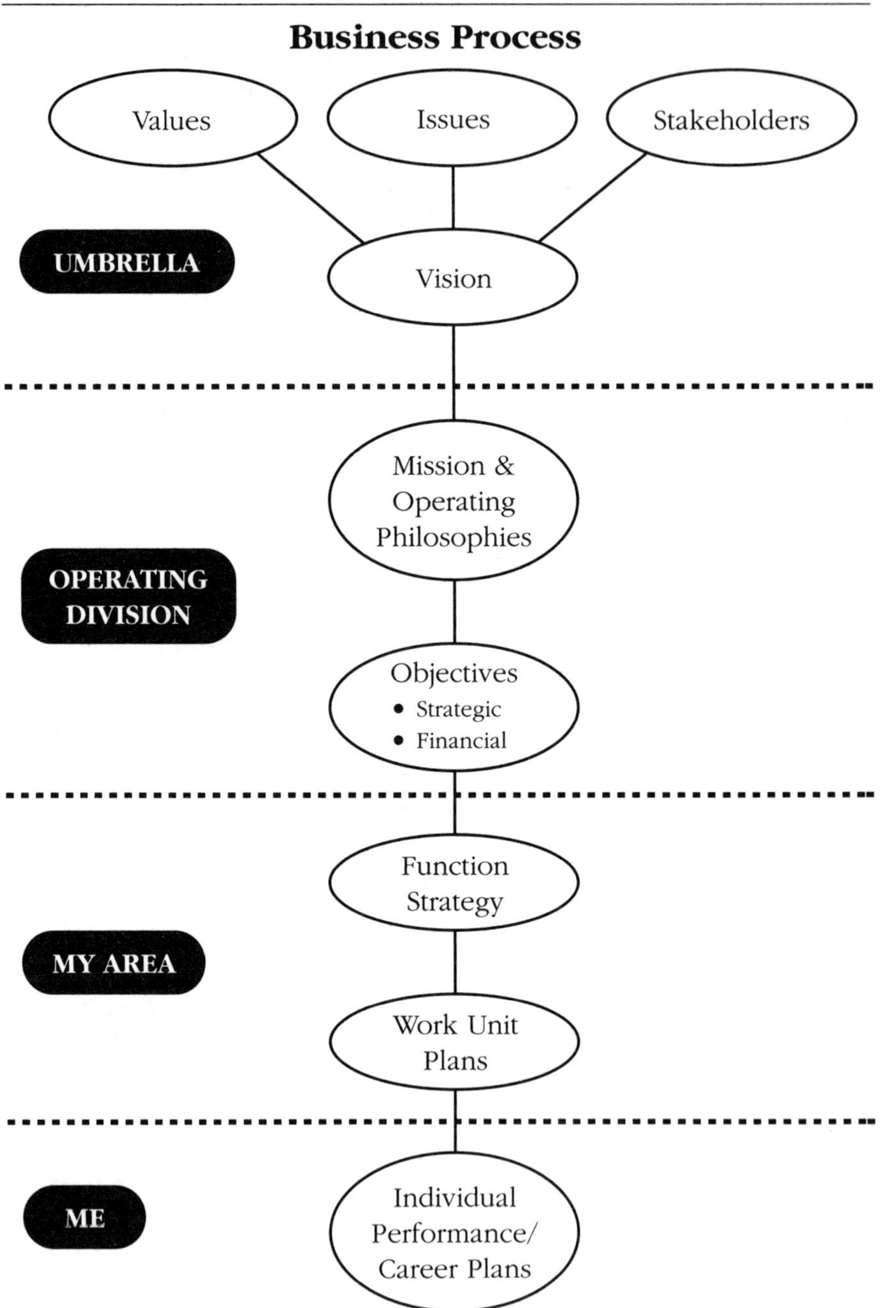

FIGURE 15: Harley-Davidson Business Process

Vision

Harley-Davidson, Inc., is an action-oriented, international company. It is a leader in its commitment to continuously improve the quality of profitable relationships with stakeholders. Harley-Davidson believes the key to success is to balance stakeholders' interests through the empowerment of all employees to focus on value-added activities.

Values

Tell the truth
Be fair
Keep your promises
Respect the individual
Encourage intellectual curiosity

Stakeholders

Stakeholders are those who could put Harley-Davidson out of business: customers, suppliers, employees, shareholders, government, and society.

Issues

Quality—Continuous improvement activities to reduce waste defects and variability in everything we do, while striving to meet/exceed customers' expectations.

Participation—Is open to influence; provides an opportunity to make a difference.

Productivity—Is effective; does the thing right; is efficient; does the right thing.

Flexibility—Rapidly and efficiently responds to changes in the internal and external environment.

Cash Flow—Necessary for longevity.

Referring to a new flattened organizational structure, described later in this chapter, Teerlink argues that companies must be driven by interdependence, not by the bottom line. He notes that the Vision Statement says nothing about profits.

Teerlink admits that the company's people have not yet grasped the totality of what these values are. He lays the blame on the company's leadership, which, starting with the CEO, must provide a compelling reason for changes in behavior and beliefs.

People generally try to do too many things and the Issues help them focus. Those Issues should be essentially the same 200 years from now. But to make values and issues live and breathe, definitions are required. Definitions of issues such as quality must be the same, or else, when people are under stress, their disagreement or misunderstanding will become apparent.

Controller Jim Brostowitz says that the umbrella and the Business Process are changing the company's culture and causing it to do things differently. For example, balancing stakeholders' interests, being fair with all the respective groups, is a big shift from the way Harley-Davidson and most other companies have viewed their objectives in the past. When Brostowitz was a CPA with a Big Six accounting firm, he never heard such a topic discussed. Aside from some discussion of how their decisions would affect labor or the shareholders, corporate managements were fixated on the bottom line. Though he admits that Harley-Davidson has not yet fully succeeded in making the Business Process work, he believes that people are considering these issues more in their business decisions.

When asked which of the company's values he considers most important, John Hevey, director of finance for Marketing Operations, says that picking one over the other was tough. However, he believes that telling the truth, being fair, and encouraging intellectual curiosity are the company values most important to the finance area. If you practice those three, mutual respect with other individuals and keeping your promises follow naturally. "Telling the truth in a finance environment is critical," Hevey says. "If you're going to blow a budget, if there is a problem in a subsidiary such as a budget error or a market turning, we need to know that. Telling the truth and building trust is particularly important on the international level where you can't walk down the hall." He adds that being fair and respecting the individual are critical values underlying long-standing partnerships, both internal and external.

Balancing Stakeholders' Interests

CEO Teerlink says that the company could increase profits by changing the allocation between domestic and international or by raising prices 10 percent, but that would not be fair to stakeholders. When he tells that to Wall Street, they don't like it, but he points out that the stock has done pretty well.

Laying off 40 percent of the employees so that the other 60 percent could stay was a poignant example of balancing stakeholder interests. Keeping every employee would not have helped the shareholders. Balance is subjective.

Teerlink believes that the company can be humane and still cut costs. Sometimes it is necessary to suboptimize. "If everything were objective we would run businesses by computers. The objective decisions are easy. You want to get a 12 percent return rather than 10. But what if you hurt a thousand families? Maybe I want to get just 10. It's a tough decision. I know I'll get beat up by the financial analysts. Do I have the courage to make the decision? Those are the decisions CEOs and department heads have to make. Am I providing value with 18 people here, and if not, what am I going to do about it?"

Intersecting Circles

The company has recently created a flattened organization of three intersecting circles (figure 16). In the Create Demand Circle, also known as the Marketing Circle, are the sales, marketing, distribution, service, styling, and brand management functions. In the Produce Products Circle, also known as the Manufacturing Circle, are the engineering and manufacturing functions. In the Support Circle are the human resources, management information systems, finance, and legal functions. In the middle ground is an executive group called the Leadership and Strategy Council. Membership consists of the president of the company and two members from each of the three circles. The president is a permanent member. Members from the circles serve two-year terms; three of the six memberships rotate every year. How the circles interact and how the middle is defined are still evolving, but John Hevey, director of finance for Marketing Operations, observes, "There was a lot of functional autonomy in the company, but now through the circle approach we are trying to build relationships and partnerships. The key is to increase the information flow among the circles."

The three-circle organization allows the finance function to be both centralized, with its core in the Support Circle, and decentralized, with finance people working in the Create Demand and Produce Products Circles. Some financial responsibilities such as borrowing and cash management are better centralized for efficiency and economies of scale. Other finance functions related to supporting line business managers are best decentralized to facilitate information sharing and close working relationships.

Figure 16: Harley-Davidson Intersecting Circles

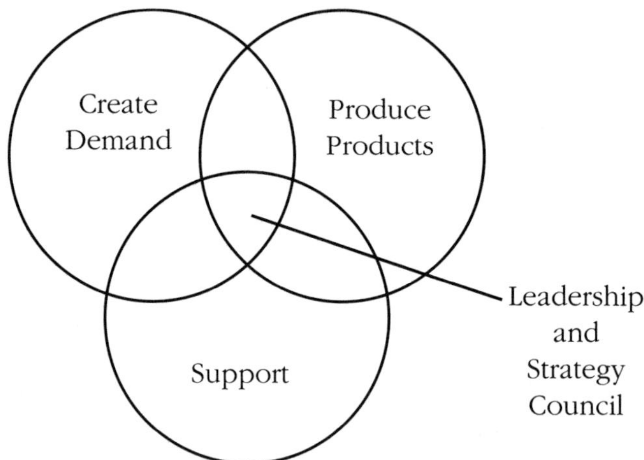

Hevey is the finance person working in the Create Demand Circle. He was previously with Ernst & Young, where he was a senior tax manager. At Harley-Davidson, he started as manager of International Finance, dealing with issues such as overseas subsidiary structure, international tax planning, transfer pricing, banking relationships, and foreign exchange exposure management. In his current assignment in the Create Demand Circle, he works with nine counterparts at the director and vice president level who are responsible for marketing, market research, sales, service, distribution, and logistics. He has been in the position for just a year and finds that the roles within the group are still being defined. He does not claim to be an expert on marketing strategy, but he is prepared to advise the group on the financing and budgeting implications of those strategies as they are being defined.

Hevey participates in strategic planning discussions, including discussions of goals for one-, three-, and five-year plans. His primary role is preparing the circle's budgets and forecasts. Before the three-circle organization was established, a financial planning group was responsible for forecasts, budgets, and plan/actual reviews. It did not work very well because the finance people had a reputation for saying too much. They were particularly vocal in recommending where budget cuts were needed. People padded their budgets because they knew the finance people would cut them back. Now financial planning is done in the three circles. Hevey, with his finance, accounting, and tax background, is participating in Marketing Circle discussions as decisions are being made. He gains an understanding through the year of why the Marketing Group wants to spend money, and he may make suggestions along the way, rather than simply reacting at budget time that the group is spending too much. As a result, finance people are now seen as advocates of the budgets rather than naysayers.

People who work for Hevey act as a service group within the Marketing Circle, helping managers and their staffs with budgets, plan/actual analysis, and other projects. Recent examples of projects have included working with the Distribution Group to develop a proposal for a new warehouse and assisting the Sales Division to prepare the justification for a dealer incentive trip, quantifying benefits such as increased parts and accessories sales and training courses for dealers. Hevey is also able to provide firsthand information to the CFO and treasurer, keeping them up to date on marketing plans and helping them understand the Marketing Circle's goals.

John Hevey frequently works with his finance counterparts in the Manufacturing and Support Circles. The three group finance directors get together to coordinate budgets, forecasts, and strategic plans. For example, demand is currently outstripping the company's manufacturing capacity, and the company must plan carefully which markets motorcycles will be shipped to. Hevey and his counterpart in manufacturing have developed a model that shows on a rolling basis, as close to real time as possible, what is scheduled to be produced, how production is doing, and the markets to which bikes will be shipped. Marketing and manufacturing people often have video conference calls to discuss the information in the reports and what actions should be taken. Hevey acts as an observer, making sure that the model he developed continues to serve its purpose.

Fence Setting: Empowerment with Boundaries

CEO Rich Teerlink asks, "How do you raise a child?" and provides a reply from Dr. Spock: "Freedom with fences." He says that you grow a successful organization in the same way, freedom with fences. To empower people, give them fences so they can be empowered. He explains that empowerment is not anarchy as some think. Without fences people become frustrated because they don't know if they are going over the line. This does not mean that they should never go over the line. But when they do, Teerlink believes that they need to know they are doing it. Unless it is an issue of time, they need to go back to the person who established the fence and talk about it. Sometimes the fence may change, sometimes not. Teerlink believes that we must get away from the notion that everybody can do everything. We all have different skills. Anxiety occurs when people don't know where their fences are and they try to do things they are not qualified to do.

Fence setting at Harley-Davidson is part of the process of defining work unit plans, individual performance plans, and where individuals are empowered to go—all within the functional strategy, objectives, and mission under the umbrella.

In the three-circle organization, there is fence setting among and within the circles. Hevey recounts that some people came into the circles with entrenched "this is what I do" attitudes. Then, in a mutual fence-setting process, they began to negotiate with each other, and authority and responsibility started to shift among functions more easily than it had in the past. Now, for example, fence setting for the Marketing Group takes place all in one room. If the sales people are developing programs that are way beyond the budget, they need to negotiate. When a function such as sales was more autonomous and there was less information flow, they could embark on a costly new program and finance would not find out about it until six months later.

Harley-Davidson sees Europe as its next big growth area. Marketing, sales, distribution, and finance are all working together as a core team in developing the strategy, rather than working on their own as four separate departments. For example, there is no floor planning in Europe, and credit terms are currently different in each country. Finance is working with marketing to develop a comprehensive customer financing strategy.

Leadership and Coaching

Although formal leaders are not appointed for each circle, coach/facilitators have assisted the groups in the beginning as they have developed their modes of operation. One of their tasks has been to help people who are accustomed to working in a traditional, hierarchical, command-and-control system adjust to a more fluid, team-oriented environment.

Business Planning Cycle

In late summer and early fall, the company starts to plan its business strategy for the next year and to revise its rolling three-year plan. When the planning process starts, dollars are not discussed. The company concentrates on large, broad items, things it wants to accomplish, directions in which it wants to go—for example, increasing capacity to 100,000 units a year. In each plant, each function, including finance, marketing, human resources, management information systems (MIS), and manufacturing tells the board what it wants to do, what its targets are, and how the targets relate to the business. The board buys in on the overall goals before it is presented with the numbers. Then, after the buy-in of the goals, the dollar budgeting process begins. The board approves the final plan and budget in the first week in December.

Controller Jim Brostowitz notes that finance is part of the process at every step. As a support function, finance people are helping the rest of the organization understand business impacts during the planning process, not after the fact. He cites a decision to switch to local-currency billing overseas as an example. In the past, marketing might have made such a decision to increase sales without considering the impact on the rest of the organization—for example, the ability of the accounts receivable system to accommodate foreign currency amounts. Now finance is part of the decision-making process from the beginning, and there are fewer surprises.

Role of the Finance Function

CEO Teerlink believes that the finance function must understand that it is a service organization. He asks, "How many people in the finance function honestly believe they have a customer other than top management?" and answers, "Very few, unfortunately!" Teerlink believes that finance people must understand that finance does not drive the organization. In this respect, he sees himself as an unconventional former CFO, but he points out that he also ran a plant for three years, and after working as a CPA he deliberately sought experience on the operating side.

Teerlink believes that when finance people get picked on, they get what they deserve. "Most finance people honestly think they run the business. They think they can run a business with numbers. The tragedy is that too many boards of directors are promoting finance people to be CEOs. They get away from the sense of people. They say, 'Here's the number,' but numbers are only outcomes of how all these people do their jobs."

He continues, "I am a firm believer that people in the finance area have to get out of the finance function for a period of their career because they don't understand what is really going on in the real world. They don't understand that the numbers are only the history of what has happened in the business. They don't try to get behind what the numbers really mean, so they end up preparing financial analyses that are very impressive for financial people but don't do a damned thing to help you run the business better."

Teerlink says, "I don't like TQM programs. They are frequently form over substance." He would rather be able to walk up to every employee and say, "Who's your customer? How does your customer measure you? What do you have in your workspace that shows how you are doing against your customer's measure? Who do you need to help you deliver what your customer wants?" "If every employee in the organization knows that, we have the greatest quality system in the world. My customer is the person who gets the output.

"The first issue of quality the finance function must ask is, 'Who is our customer?' The customer is not the outside world. The customer is not top management. They get the output. But the most important customers are those within the organization who are preparing budgets and incurring costs. Finance people need to help them understand the financial impact of their actions, and not just with a negative variance report, which is what most financial people do. Most accountants get great delight telling people how they have done poorly, and that they haven't met their budgets, and then beating them up and telling them they have to do better."

Teerlink commented on how to get finance people to focus on process rather than results, and whether this might be in conflict with their objectivity. "What's objectivity? A number? Let's be honest; the biggest estimate in the world is the audited financial statements that are presented to the public. And the auditor's opinion says so. They're sort of right, and there's nothing wrong with that. Let's recognize what it is rather than thinking it's precise to the penny, which is the implication. I think you have to develop systems within the organization that are driven at other levels than the senior level. I think it is very important to have program budgeting so people truly understand where their money is going and can make decisions."

He believes that fully allocated costs are misleading, particularly those relating to "ready-to-serve" costs. Ready-to-serve costs are fixed costs the company incurs just to stay in business. There are costs in the finance function that do not apply to any real program. They are there because the company has, for example, a controller. Teerlink looks at each one of these ready-to-serve costs and asks if it is really needed.

"The major task of the finance function is to help people understand what our value-added activities are. That's a major task. If it doesn't add value somewhere we shouldn't incur the costs. Finding that out requires a whole lot of time talking to people. I don't have to measure it. I just feel good about some things.

"As a finance guy you have to come into the real world where people exist. People exist in the soft world. The companies that make a difference and do well today are not the companies that Harold Geneen built. They are the companies that care and understand what the soft issues are, and they have leaders who believe in stewardship.

"The finance function exists at the pleasure of those it serves. It is not a line organization, but a good one should operate that way. It supports the line and helps it do its job better. Its a service organization and that's the most important thing. Finance people can help others understand what is value added by just talking to them.

"Max DePree says there are three things a leader should do. The first is to define reality, the second is to be a steward, and the third is to say thank-you. How many finance people believe that, other than the reality that you're no damn good and I have the numbers to show you? And that's wrong, because does that build a team? Does that build cooperation? Does that build a spirit of one?"

Control Through Accountability

In the past, travel and entertainment expenses were reviewed and questioned by supervisors and then sent to control, where a clerk would review them, adding and subtracting and looking at receipts, perhaps pointing out, "You spent too much on dinner." This doesn't fit the new culture, and the control function has stopped doing it. Jim Brostowitz points out that accounting and finance can't make the decision on what's appropriate, so they shouldn't try. It's a conversation for the supervisor and employee to have, and there is a policy manual that spells out what people should and should not spend. There are now built-in soft controls that work through people being accountable. Though this is not the only thing the company relies on, it is a step in the right direction, and it makes a controller such as Brostowitz more comfortable than the old way.

Leadership Training

The company believes that its primary sustainable competitive advantage is people. Therefore, it has developed a strong internal training and development program. This program is operated through the Harley-Davidson Leadership Institute, which provides topic-specific seminars, technical skills courses, college credit courses, and a leadership series. Everyone in the company attends certain topic-specific seminars such as empowerment. A two-day seminar covers how to set fences, deal with other staff members, and push down responsibilities. People in leadership positions are attending a leadership series, which has three elements. First is putting values into action. As noted by

Peter Senge in *The Fifth Discipline,* you need to get in touch with yourself to contribute to an organization. Teerlink believes that most people are not in touch with themselves and do not know what is important to them. In this part of the seminar, individuals attempt to clarify their personal values and connect them with Harley-Davidson's values. The second part is a four-and-a-half-day program entitled "Leadership Fundamentals" that focuses on skills related to interaction and execution. Last is another four-and-a-half-day program devoted to functional excellence, which provides insight into what is considered leading-edge thinking in the major functional areas of the business.

Hiring Finance Professionals

In hiring professional people in finance and other functions, the company looks for a balance. Education and technical skills are important, but no more important than "what the person is like." Everyone who interviews and hires attends behavioral interviewing seminars, which help prospective employers look at the positions they are trying to fill and what skills are needed.

Cross-Functional Job Rotation

Harley-Davidson encourages its executives to move around and get experience in different functions. Rich Teerlink cites one vice president who was in charge of financial planning at the time of the LBO, then controller, then in charge of marketing, then the motorcycle group, and back to marketing. Jeff Bleustein, president of the Motorcycle Group, ran engineering, then parts and accessories, then international, and then was in a special assignment in operations. It is the company's desire for moves such as these be the rule rather than the exception, and it feels that through the Leadership Institute and the career development effort they will become the rule. This should help executives from functions such as finance become well-rounded general managers and facilitate working relationships among the company's three intersecting circles.

8

Geo. E. Keith Company

Interview Subjects: *Jeffrey A. Weber, president; Hitesh Amin, controller; David Harrington, treasurer*

Executive Summary

The Geo. E. Keith story illustrates the role of changing values and the leadership of the finance function in a company turnaround. The former management believed that company tradition and employee devotion to product quality could be the foundation for rescuing an underperforming shoe manufacturer. The current CEO is a finance person acting as cultural change agent. His values relate to internal working relationships. They include being honest and fair with people, not allowing any person or group to receive preferential treatment, and avoiding politics. This case shows how teamwork, information sharing, organizational learning, and internal and external partnerships can help a small company pull through a period of financial difficulty. The treasurer and the controller assume broad responsibilities going beyond traditional financial roles. They work on teams with other functions such as manufacturing, marketing, and product development to make pricing, costing, and production planning decisions. A weekly flash report of key financial information helps maintain credibility both inside the company and with external partners such as bankers, vendors, and suppliers.

Background

The Geo. E. Keith Shoe Company of Bridgewater, Massachusetts, is the oldest shoe company in the United States. It traces its history back to 1758 in a community close to the Plymouth settlement. At the turn of the century, the company was one of the largest shoe manufacturers in the world. It had retail stores throughout the United States and in London and Paris as well. There were 20 manufacturing plants in the vicinity of Brockton, Massachusetts. Over the years, along with the rest of the industry, the company was affected by foreign competition, and it downsized to its present single plant in Bridgewater.

In the late 1980s, under previous owners, the company was making about half a dozen types of shoes with retail prices under $100, including dirty bucks and traditional men's dress shoes. They were sold throughout the United States, primarily to independent shoe stores, but also to some department stores and private brand resellers. The company had $10 to $12 million in sales and was profitable.

The company was put up for sale and purchased in an LBO in March 1990. The investor group included a CEO with success in turning around other companies and some well-known names in venture capital, retailing, apparel, and the shoe industry. The investors saw in Geo. E. Keith an opportunity to build on company values, a sense of history, and a solid reputation for quality.

Business Strategy Following LBO

After the LBO, the company's new management made substantial changes in the company's product and marketing strategy. It expanded the product line, targeted a higher priced market, and developed department store distribution channels. The Walk-Over brand had been sold primarily to independent stores in the Northeast at a price point of $100 and below. A new strategy was centered on a premium product selling for $120 to $170 in large apparel and department store chains such as Neimann Marcus, Brooks Brothers, Nordstrom's, and Dillard's. The company started to sell in new markets such as California. They hired a well-known designer to develop higher fashion items such as suede loafers and a line of women's shoes, and placed less emphasis on traditional standbys such as welted Oxfords and dirty bucks. The company did not walk away from its relationships with the independents, but it cut its existing product line substantially and made it obvious that it was primarily interested in the large chains and big distribution channels.

To establish the brand as quickly as possible, the company hired a number of new senior sales people at relatively high fixed salaries. A substantial amount was spent on marketing. Elegant, award-winning catalogues geared to the history of the company were produced. The Geo. E. Keith shoe box was redesigned. The unit cost of the new box was $1.35 compared to $.50 before.

To this day, it is recognized that the previous management did many positive things for Geo. E. Keith, such as enhancing the brand identity and developing valuable new distribution channels. But the company's performance did not go according to plan. Though new business grew, overall revenues did not change. Overhead increased substantially, causing large losses and depleting capital. The company lost the confidence of its investors.

In retrospect, it appears that management was trying to change the company too quickly in order to satisfy the venture capitalists with fast returns. Jeff Weber, the current CEO, observes that changing a brand such as Walk-Over from a low price to premium product takes a number of years. He believes that if such a change can ever be successful, it must be made gradually, and it requires a lot of resources and skilled people.

Financial Difficulty and Management Transition

Jeff Weber joined the company two years ago as chief financial officer, with responsibility for manufacturing, finance, and all the other day-to-day inside activities while the former CEO concentrated on his areas of expertise, marketing, and selling. As the new CFO, Weber found a number of problems, including high overhead and excess inventory. He reduced operating expenses from $4.5 million to $2 million per year, remarking, "That does not go down easily." Inventory was $6.5 million compared with annual revenue of $12 million, primarily because of excess finished goods built on spec. Weber embarked on a program to gradually sell off excess inventory that continues to this day.

Hitesh Amin, controller, and Dave Harrington, treasurer, were both hired by the former CEO. Both had relevant experience in larger companies and saw an opportunity to grow in a smaller, more entrepreneurial environment.

Amin is responsible for accounting and taxes but is also comfortable in the factory and working with development people. He has been a key player in costing out the product. His earlier experience was with an appliance manufacturer in England and then with a systems consulting firm in New England.

Harrington's responsibilities include credit and collection, customer service, and warehousing and distribution. He works on a daily basis with bankers, customers, the sales force, and the factory. He is as comfortable outside the company as he is inside. His job ranges from giving bankers factory tours to working with retail customers to make sure the product is delivered on time. Previously, Harrington worked in the treasury group and was responsible for banking relationships at Timberland.

Back-to-Basics Strategy

Geo. E. Keith's current business is a mix of private label and branded products. It is working hard to reestablish its branded business in the United States. Private label business is necessary because it provides a financial base. In addition to Reebok and Rockport, the company makes all of the buck and saddle shoes for L. L. Bean, Armani, Faconnable, Neimann Marcus, Brooks Brothers, and Cole Haan. Ten percent of the company's sales are in dollars through a New York trading company to customers in Japan, where they have a strong reputation.

When Dave Harrington joined the company as treasurer, he had no experience in production planning. He started by asking basic questions about what the company was making and why. It turned out that raw materials were purchased and shoes were made based on sales people's forecasts. High inventory was already one of the company's serious problems. With the manufacturing and sales people, Harrington reexamined the production planning cycle. They decided that the company should focus on 10 basic styles and never be out of stock. The company narrowed down its product line substantially but offered each model in more sizes and widths. Retailers are now told, "This will always be in stock. It will always be available. You call and we'll have it to you in two or three days." The company is concentrating on the traditional styles for which it has been well known in the past, and not trying to be a fashion leader. It is trying to get people both externally and internally to understand what it is all about and what it sells.

CFO as Cultural Change Agent

Jeff Weber describes the former CFO and controller as a good person who was in over her head. The former CEO had more of a marketing orientation and in Weber's opinion underestimated the CFO's job; he thought it was an accounting job that he did not have to worry about. Investors wanted a full-fledged financial person in the CFO role. When Weber joined the company, he assumed responsibility for production as well, becoming in effect the chief operating officer.

During his first year, Weber made a lot of changes. As the CFO, between the investors and the CEO he had to walk a fine line, making sure he did things that were best for the company. The sales team had been viewed as the engine that drove the company, but Weber thought that the sales team compensation packages were out of line with the industry and the size of the company and were a source of poor morale among other people in the company. Production and finance people felt they were being blamed for all of the problems while the sales people were receiving favored treatment. People in the factory felt that promises were made and not kept. Management was uncomfortable dealing with the internal tension and conflict caused by the company's rapid transition and concentrating more on getting out and developing new business. As a CFO with more of an internal focus, Weber saw the need for team building among the company's various functions.

Role of the Finance Function in Management

Weber sees financial people as falling into three classifications: "typical bean counters," people with strong analytical skills who can also relate to what's going on in the company, and business people. A company needs a person who closes the books, but it also needs people who can bridge gaps and understand the business.

One of the hardest jobs a financial person has is managing upward. A CFO has to try to present the CEO with a balanced picture of what is going on, where the problems are, and what needs to be done. Financial reports are not enough. The CFO has to work with the heads of marketing, sales, product development, and manufacturing to represent their interests and explain the story behind the numbers. The former CFO was an accountant who did not know how to deal with the more marketing-oriented CEO. As the company began to lose money, the only approach she knew was to curtail spending. She did not understand how to work with the other function heads to analyze the problems, or how to ask the CEO if marketing money could be spent more effectively instead of asking him to cut spending.

Weber observes that companies can make their biggest mistakes when they are growing, and poor cost management is buried by ever-improving results. It is difficult for the finance person to argue against success. If growth is managed effectively, the company is better prepared for the inevitable downturn. A finance person is in a more powerful position in a turnaround when the issue is survival, but the job is still difficult because not everybody agrees on what has to be done.

New Values

Given the background of this traditional New England company, it would be hard to disagree with values such as a sense of history and the quality of the product. The current management has tried to capitalize on those values while concentrating on three behavioral principles: Be honest and fair with people; no one group is better than anyone else; politics has no place. Following these principles and bonding the company together as a team is the foundation of Jeff Weber's survival strategy.

Being honest and fair is a particular challenge for a company in financial difficulty. Weber has tried to tell people whether or not they are doing the right job and to keep them informed. He has told the company staff that some good things may be developing, but that there are still tough times ahead. He has tried to get more people involved, getting them to make suggestions on how to change things. Before the LBO, the factory was run by the autocratic approach of, "Do your job, do what you are told, and keep quiet." Then, after the LBO, the company was driven primarily by the sales function. Now, Weber has told the staff that no one person or group can lead the company out of its problems. He has tried to persuade people to forget past grudges and start working as a team, warning that people who won't work together aren't going to be there anymore.

The company cannot appear to be doing more for its sales force, marketing team, or finance team than it is doing for its factory workers. Sales may be crucial to the company's future, but if the factory workers can't make the product properly, the distribution people can't get it out the door and to the customer on time, and the finance people can't price to the point where it's going to make money, then sales doesn't matter. Granted, there are different levels of pay, but here again management must be honest and fair with each employee. Weber believes that there have been a lot of inequities in the company because of personal biases in the past, but also that rectifying them takes time. He can't reevaluate everybody's job and change their pay all at once. He is trying to identify the worst cases and solve those initially.

Politics can be particularly damaging in a small company, unlike a larger company where jockeying for position and power is a way of life. That is why Weber and a number of his associates such as Amin and Harrington like being where they are. People feel they can deal openly and honestly with each other. Dress is informal. The atmosphere is low key. People are trying to work together to get the job done and make the company successful. They know that what they are trying to accomplish will not be easy and that they are essentially starting at the bottom.

Rebuilding the Company as a Team

Jeff Weber has concentrated on making the whole company work as a team, forging working relationships so that everything does not have to come through him. He has encouraged manufacturing, finance, and product development people to work together to understand how costs can be reduced and how the company's products can be priced effectively.

When Weber first met and talked with the company's key players, they said they did not know what their jobs were. One day it was one thing; another day it was another. People appeared to be pigeonholed in their positions without any understanding of how they fit in. They asked for an organization chart. Weber worked with them to redefine roles, trying to emphasize people's strengths and to get people to do more than they were asked—a way of life in a small company. Everybody had some ideas on what had to be done with the company.

In the beginning, before moving into a private office, Weber sat in a high-traffic area. He got to know people quickly and learned that they were open and willing to say what was on their minds. If there were problems in the factory or the warehouse, a lack of orders or even a tight cash position, everyone knew it. This was good and bad, but at least everybody was interested and wanted to be involved.

At this point, the company has cut back supervisory positions, and a number of people are doing jobs below their skill sets. An assistant plant manager is running the stitching room as well as finishing and packing. The person responsible for quality and development is also running the lasting and making operations.

Unfortunately, asking people to take on additional responsibility during a difficult period delays other matters management would rather attend to. Weber would like to devote more of his efforts to building teamwork throughout the company, increasing job mobility, and bringing in more young people for training. He explains that far more skill is required in a shoe company than in a typical manufacturing company. Assuming he can make the business viable, Weber's longer term goal is to have people compensated based on a piece rate and manage themselves, and have managers concentrate more on quality. He believes that people have tremendous knowledge and ability, and, if treated this way, will find ways to improve productivity and to change things. By contrast, he believes that if people are paid on an hourly basis, they must be managed and will do more or less work depending on what they are given.

Teamwork in the Finance Function

A three-person accounting department, led by an accounting manager, reports to Hitesh Amin, controller. The department does the company's accounting and bookkeeping, accounts payable, accounts receivable, and payroll. Within that group, everything is done more or less on a team basis. Everyone knows his responsibility and can always ask for help. Amin leaves them alone most of the time but tries to ask them how they think things can be improved, and to get them involved whenever possible in the decision process.

Systems, production planning, and inventory all have their control aspects. Amin has a lot of prior experience in systems, and he gets involved as part of a team in troubleshooting, understanding what the problems are, and helping choose and implement a new system. Because it is a small company, everyone is dependent on everyone else, unlike a company with big accounting, marketing, and MIS staffs, where people may work primarily on their own to demonstrate their capabilities. Here, people must be willing to work together as a team and try things they have never done before.

As an example of finance working with the factory as a team, Amin cites a problem in the stitching department. There was a high turnover of knives, and stitching was taking longer than it should have. He and his staff evaluated the problem, working as a team with the purchasing department, and developed a solution. They discovered that buying better quality knives would reduce cost in the long run. Finance people cannot just sit at their desks and figure out why costs are going up or down. There are a lot of hidden costs in the factory. The only effective way for finance people to identify and reduce these costs is to get people from other functions such as manufacturing and purchasing involved in the process.

Cost Accounting

The former CEO's approach to product costing was to figure out what the retail price and retailer's price margin should be, what Geo. E. Keith should charge for the shoes, and then figure out how to get there. This approach is widely used in many industries, but Weber does not agree with it. He believes in making to a standard, not a price. This requires starting with the design, costing it out, figuring out the margin, developing a price point, and seeing if retailers can sell for that. If they can't, you go back and look at the shoe again and see if you can make any adjustments. This is a bottom-up rather than top-down approach. Shoes require different amounts of labor, material, and overhead. For example, a wingtip with perforations, calfskin uppers, leather soles, and leather lining requires substantially more time and effort than a dirty buck.

Before Amin joined the company, every product had the same labor and overhead cost. Material was the only variable cost. However, different types of shoes require different amounts of time. A true standard cost would require an industrial engineer to analyze every function and process and determine exactly how much time it takes. The company didn't have the time or resources to do that. Amin formed a team with people from manufacturing and finance to establish five levels of difficulty for the company's product line. A shoe absorbs a labor and overhead rate according to its level of difficulty. The cost of the shoe is calculated accordingly. This allows the company to calculate a margin for each shoe and to figure out whether it can be profitable at a given price point.

Now, when costing out each new shoe, Amin continues to coordinate with factory, product development, and marketing people. A marketing person or customer wants a particular product. A product development person writes specifications. Amin works with manufacturing to determine the level of difficulty and how the new product will fit into the total flow of production. They decide together whether all product requirements can be fulfilled in house, or whether it would be cheaper for parts of the shoe to be made somewhere else. If a shoe requires more than the usual amount of stitching, Amin goes to the stitching department and discusses the required number of operations.

Marketing, product development, manufacturing, and the controller are all involved in setting prices, with the eventual consent of sales and approval by the president. In deciding what to charge the retailer, the company must compare the internal unit cost with the retail price points. Based on market intelligence such as what competitors are offering, the product and pricing strategy is reevaluated every season. The company also takes into account plant capacity, the backlog of orders, and the amount of private label business it is doing. Manufacturing and production planning people must always be involved in the process. If there is excess capacity, they may offer price breaks, or if they don't have much capacity, they may ask for a premium. The cost is never exact, and decisions must often be made quickly. It is important to do a good estimate but not to waste time trying to be unrealistically accurate.

Information Sharing

Jeff Weber believes that the more people know and the more they understand about the business, the better they can do their jobs. He has encouraged informal communication within the company and improved financial reports to help internal managers, investors, and bankers understand the business. Information has been shared selectively with suppliers as well.

Informal communication has improved as people in various functions have learned to work together. Sales people are giving better feedback on what is selling. Aside from a weekly staff meeting, the company does not have many formal meetings. Except for the sales staff, people are all working in one place. Everyone is accessible.

Weber has begun circulating a report to all sales people that shows the top 10 selling shoes, margins by product line, who is selling what, and the dollar volume sold to each account, including retailers and private label customers. He also sends them weekly reports showing each person's order rate and ranking their performance. Reactions have been mixed. Some have been defensive. Others have used the information as a tool to do their jobs better, for example, paying more attention to certain products or customers. The company's systems are not yet capable of producing a profit and loss statement by customer. That will be included in a new financial reporting system the company is designing and installing with the help of government funding.

Despite its financial constraints, the company is investing in new systems to improve information flow in the factory and to improve communication with customers and suppliers. Now, information is outdated when it is received in the factory. Checking inventory and telling customers when their orders will be shipped is time-consuming. Production must sometimes be stopped because the leather did not arrive on time.

Partnerships are being established with customers and suppliers to implement Quick Response and electronic data interchange (EDI). In the factory, a bar-code system is being developed so that people will know what production goes from one room to the next and can calculate the piece rate and track inventory continuously on a daily rather than weekly or snapshot basis. Disseminating information through better systems will decentralize decision making. Treasurer Dave Harrington believes that when these systems are in place, it will be more feasible for people to work in self-managed teams and be accountable for their own performance. The objective is to make everyone feel part of a team and responsible for something.

Flash Reports

Hitesh Amin has developed a weekly flash report that shows how every manager and supervisor and the whole company performed for the previous week, for the month, and for the year to date. It includes information such as sales, production, inventory, orders received, shipments, labor cost, and the factory damage (FD) rate. There are ratios such as inventory to sales. There is an ABC classification relating 80 percent of the inventory to 80 percent of sales, by account. The reports are prepared by the accounting group and shared with all managers so that they have a common information base to help them discuss problems and issues. The reports are also sent to the investors every week.

External Partnerships

Part of Dave Harrington's job is sharing information with banks, suppliers, and retailers. He gives the banks a weekly report that includes financials and orders received and keeps them abreast of efforts to cut costs and build volume and backlog. He believes that he has improved relationships with the banks by trying to be up front and represent the company with integrity. Recently, the company had monthly meetings with its banks; now they are required only quarterly. Coming from a banking background, Harrington is surprised at how supportive the banks have been. He believes that the company has an appeal as one of the few remaining shoe companies in New England. The BayBanks people appear to simply like the company and want to see it survive.

Sharing information and timing payments to suppliers is a delicate process. When a company is paying 90 days slow, word gets around quickly. Harrington has tried to work carefully with each vendor, telling them when they will receive payments, providing some information on how the company is doing, but not telling them how bleak things really are. He held a special meeting with the company's top 10 suppliers, telling them, "We need you, we want to be honest with you, and we want you to be able to work with us." They appreciated it. Nobody has cut off the company. Some have applied pressure to work balances down when the company has exceeded its credit limits. Some weeks, Harrington has to make careful decisions when he can only pay one or two vendors.

Vendor relations are important for other reasons as well. Vendors keep the company informed about different leathers, and they react to feedback when the company has problems with their material.

Sharing information with retailers, particularly the independents, has not been easy. The company still has a credibility problem when it promises to support the small stores that it hurt over the last couple of years. Now the company once again has the right product in sufficient supply and has to ask the retailers to give it an honest chance. Frank information exchange with large private label customers such as L. L. Bean is equally important. Harrington has kept them apprised of the company's financial condition and related information such as investors' plans to advance more funds. Customers have been reassuring in return, saying that they want the company to survive, that it is their best source of welted shoes, and that they do not have to "QC" the shoes they received.

An open dialogue and the weekly flash report have improved the working relationship with the two key investors.

Organizational Learning

Hitesh Amin believes that the biggest learning curve has involved getting people to speak the same language. Management did not come from a shoe manufacturing background. People in the factory spoke a shoe language. There was a lack of communication and understanding about the processes of manufacturing. Manufacturing people found it difficult to think financially or talk about issues related to the organization as a whole. Management had to talk at their level and get their feedback concerning the effect of productivity on profitability and the need to reduce costs in certain areas.

Empowerment

Jeff Weber believes that people are empowered when they do not feel threatened by the way you work with them, and when they all have the same goal to make the company successful. This is different from doing something because your boss told you to. The company management is working hard to say, "Does it make sense to you? If so, let's do it. If not, let's talk about it." It is a major change at Geo. E. Keith because prior to the LBO, the company was run by one person who made all the decisions, including wages for every worker. Now, although people in the company are not resisting change, they are not used to it. For example, when a plant manager was asked to recommend salary increases, he confessed he had never known how much any of his people earned.

Weber encourages decision making in a group setting. As a manager, he feels strongly about delegating people the power to do their jobs. He says, "If you have hired the right people, they will get the job done for you." But if there is a problem or an important issue, he expects people to come and talk about it.

Open discussion and teamwork are an important part of his strategy to improve the company's financial condition.

9
Herman Miller, Inc.

Interview Subjects: *James H. Bloem, vice president and chief financial officer; James E. Christenson, vice president and chief counsel*

Executive Summary

The Herman Miller story is one of leadership principles such as participative management, covenants with employees, and equity and fairness that were instilled two generations ago and have been continuously practiced and refined since then. It is a story of a group of people who consider how they work together and how they satisfy the customer to be just as important as the company's financial results and their own compensation.

At Herman Miller, good technical skills in finance are assumed. Most people hired have already developed those skills working for other companies. To succeed at Herman Miller, finance people need to develop organizational, influencing, and interpersonal skills and a well-rounded knowledge of the business. That business knowledge comes from a career ladder that is more horizontal than vertical. Finance people learn by rotating through functions such as sales, product design, distribution, and logistics, as well as financial disciplines such as public accounting, cost accounting, audit, control, credit, and general ledger.

Finance people must deal with ambiguity. There are no hard-and-fast criteria by which business decisions are made. Decisions involve a number of people from different functions and a lengthy negotiating process. Finance people can help settle disputes among different functions in the company by maintaining their impartiality. They act as facilitators, but not arbitrators. When decisions are made, the reasons are always explained to the people concerned.

Herman Miller is more an assembler than a manufacturer. Competitive pressure in the industry makes the company's partnerships with its suppliers and dealers particularly important. Confidence and trust are important criteria for such relationships.

Background

Headquartered in Zeeland, Michigan, the company originated as the Star Furniture Company in 1905. In 1923, the company was purchased by a new group that included D. J. DePree, CEO, and his father-in-law, Herman Miller, substantial shareholder and company namesake. The company manufactured traditional-style home furniture until the mid-1930s, when it began to work with well-known contemporary designers such as Gilbert Rohde, Charles Eames, George Nelson, Robert Propst, and Bill Stumpf. Eames's work, including a famous molded plywood lounge chair and ottoman, is on permanent display at the Museum of Modern Art in New York City. Today, Herman Miller produces modern home furniture and a broad line of case goods, ergonomic seating, open-plan office systems, and accessories for work and health-care environments.

Herman Miller has grown rapidly in the past 25 years, from sales of less than $20 million to nearly $900 million. During that time, it has tried not to lose its small-company spirit. Many people in leadership positions today have come through the finance function, and people in the finance function are continuing to move into general management positions. The former CEO, Dick Ruch, was CFO before that, and also served as vice president of manufacturing and vice president of administration during his 35-year career.

DePree on Leadership

D. J. DePree was ahead of his time in setting a tone for participative management by implementing measures such as an incentive-based bonus plan. His management principles were carried on by his son

Hugh and then his younger son Max, who served as CEO until 1988. Today, Max teaches and remains chairman. No company has documented its principles and values more eloquently or fully. Max's management thinking is embodied in two highly regarded books, *Leadership Is an Art* and *Leadership Jazz.*

Max DePree believes that the most effective contemporary management style is participative management. It begins with a belief in the potential of people. Everyone has the right to influence decision making and understand the results. With participative management, decisions are not arbitrary, secret, or closed to questioning. He outlines five premises for participative management:

- Respect people and their diversity, and recognize that everyone comes with certain gifts.
- What we believe precedes policy and practice.
- Everyone has the right to be needed, involved, and to make a commitment.
- Relationships count more than structure.
- Contractual and covenantal relationships are different.

DePree explains that a contractual relationship cover things such as compensation, working conditions, benefits, rules, and job deadlines. Covenants, on the other hand, bind people together and enable them to meet their corporate needs by meeting one anothers' needs. Leaders owe their organizations covenants that serve as reference points for what caring, purposeful, committed people can be. Covenantal relationships rest on shared commitment to ideas, issues, values, and goals. They enable work to have meaning. They allow personal freedom. They encourage corporations to be hospitable to unusual people and unusual ideas, to tolerate risk and to forgive errors. They encourage participation and the formation of inclusive rather than exclusive groups.

Values are a corporation's lifeblood, but without effective communication, they will disappear in a sea of trivial memos. The best way to communicate a company's values is through behavior.

DePree believes that capitalism has been primarily an exclusive system, built around contractual relationships. Most people do not get the opportunity to be meaningfully involved in the working of the system. Exclusiveness breeds selfishness.

He says that we need to eliminate the discontinuity between how we see ourselves as persons and as workers. We can do this by translating our personal values into our daily work practices and achieving intimacy with our jobs. With intimacy, we appreciate the need to understand not just the skill but the art of a job.

DePree observes that relationships within corporations are healthiest when information is shared accurately and freely. It is better to err on the side of sharing too much information than to risk leaving someone in the dark. Information is power, but it is pointless power if hoarded. Power must be shared for an organization or relationship to work. Everyone has the right to receive and the obligation to give simplicity and clarity in communication. Only through good communication can we preserve a common corporate vision.

In 1991, Dick Ruch, Max's successor as CEO, issued a comprehensive Vision Statement (figure 17) including values, expectations, goals, and strategies. He says that its purpose is to build on the values and accomplishments of the past, but to recognize the need to manage change, to become an organization of life-long learners, to place new emphasis on continuous improvement, to reconsider the materials taken from and returned to the environment, to implement new knowledge about customer and investor needs, and to consider the whole person, including family and community relationships.

FIGURE 17: **Vision Statement**

Our Values: Who We Are

We are a company that values

- ☐ Individuals and their diversity.
  - Diversity is fundamental to success.
  - We believe in the integrity, dignity, and potential of every person.
  - Every individual's job is important.
  - All work can be rewarding and enjoyable.
- ☐ Ownership, participation, and teamwork.
  - Participation and teamwork are the best way to manage a business.
  - Ownership is essential to participation.
  - Open communication is vital to success.
  - Managers lead best by serving.

- ☐ Excellence.
  - Striving to be the best in our work, ideas, relationships, facilities, and practices is the best demonstration of our commitment to customer satisfaction.
  - Integrity and accountability must never be compromised.
  - Work well done should be celebrated and recognized.
- ☐ Social and environmental responsibility.
- ☐ Learning, good design, and new ideas.
  - Research and good design can deliver superior products and services that improve the quality of life.
  - Openness to change, innovation, risk, and failure is fundamental to our future success.
  - There is always room to improve our results and competency through personal growth.
- ☐ Equity.
  - We believe in equity for our customers, investors, vendors, dealers, and ourselves.
  - Excellent financial results are essential to the growth and vitality of our business.
  - Stewardship of resources is everyone's responsibility.

Our Expectations: The Way We Work Together

We are an organization of people who expect each other to

- ☐ Demonstrate personal integrity, competence, and commitment to excellence.
- ☐ Participate and be held accountable for results.
  - We expect to be involved in the planning, organization and control of our work and to take responsibility for its implementation.
  - We expect our actions to demonstrate trust, respect for others, and a commitment to shared values and a common vision.
  - We expect individuals and work teams to collaborate on resolution of cross-functional issues.
  - We expect managers to be open, enabling, accessible, and empowering.
- ☐ Work toward an equitable return for investors, including ourselves.

Our Goals: What We Are Working Toward

We are committed to becoming

- ☐ Our customers' reference point for excellence in service and quality.
  - Our customers should feel exceptionally well served.
  - Our products and services should improve the quality of life, sustain the environment, and merge technology and art.
  - We should provide our products at a competitive cost.

FIGURE 17: Vision Statement (continued)

- ☐ A dynamic organization where research, innovation, and good design extend to every business and function.
  - People who embrace learning, growth, change, and renewal.
  - An organization always in a state of becoming.
  - A company that will always seek better ideas, ways, and results.
- ☐ An excellent investment opportunity.

Our Strategies: How We Intend to Achieve Our Goals

We intend to achieve our vision by:

- ☐ Customer-perceived quality.
- ☐ Increased share of the market.
- ☐ Good financial results.
- ☐ Becoming a world-class competitor, marketing products in the countries that provide the best opportunities.

Satisfying Customers and Financial Results

This is a company that believes that financial results are results and not ends. CFO Jim Bloem explains, "We don't set out to achieve financial objectives. We set out to introduce new products and to satisfy customers. If we do all of that well, we will get a good financial result. We have good financial controls to ensure that we don't stray far from the mark on the down side. We have budgets and aligning processes that compare well to the rest of the world." Bloem points out that good financial discipline is in every employee's interest, because the value of the company's stock is an important part of the employee's compensation and net worth. He adds that people are generally more inspired to exceed goals such as good design and customer satisfaction than drier, strictly quantitative goals.

Organization of the Finance Function

Herman Miller has a substantial financial staff in its Zeeland, Michigan, headquarters office and in each of its product and geographic divisions. The number of people in the headquarters office doing purely financial work has been reduced from about 125 to 80 in the past five years—part of an effort that has put the company at the top of its industry in sales per employee. Routine functions have been automated, and the remaining jobs have higher skill sets and analytical content.

Seven directors in the finance function report to Jim Schreiber, controller. Those directors are responsible for accounting, internal audit, cost and profitability analysis, corporate reporting, planning, and budgeting. The assistant treasurer is also a director. Schreiber, who is also responsible for MIS, and Jim Christenson, general counsel, report to Jim Bloem, CFO, who also serves as treasurer. Bloem, Schreiber, and Christenson act as a troika; any one of the three can make a decision on behalf of the finance function in the absence of the other two.

About one-third of the finance professionals in the company, including many at the director level, are in positions tied to subsidiaries and other nonfinancial functions such as marketing, manufacturing, and logistics. The finance function plays an influencing, not a policing role. None of the subsidiary finance positions reports to finance in the head office. Finance directors work on a daily basis with, and are evaluated and paid by, the managers who run those business units and subsidiaries. However, the head office finance function does maintain a close and influential relationship with each subsidiary and business unit in order to coordinate overall financial policies and to ensure companywide financial consistency.

How the CFO Supports the CEO

J. Kermit Campbell, CEO, considers himself the company's strategist and Jim Bloem, CFO, the asset manager. Campbell prefers to concentrate on the core of the company's mission, product development and customer satisfaction, and generally is not involved from day to day in matters such as capital budgeting and talking to the financial community. But to concentrate in that way, he requires Jim Bloem to be his financial reality check, helping him implement his vision and turn it into a strategic plan. Bloem worries about things like contracts and compliance, and tells Campbell about financial matters he needs to know.

Campbell's style has fit the organization well. Before he came on board, there was internal and external concern about how well a new CEO from the outside would adapt to Herman Miller's decision-making style and whether he might try to change it. For example, manufacturing was used to deciding what equipment to buy, perhaps negotiating for expenditure approval, not being told what to do by someone outside the function. Similarly, product development and marketing people were used to working together to figure out what products would sell, not being told.

Finance People in Cross-Functional Teams

This company has had a long history of working as teams, not as functions. At any time, there could be as many as 30 cross-functional teams in operation. Most teams are formed to deal with specific problems such as warranty or service problems and are disbanded when those problems are solved. For example, a team figured out how to deliver goods shipped from throughout the United States to Los Angeles–area customers after the 1994 earthquake. An example of a warranty problem might be pilling in a furniture fabric. Finance people might be involved in investigating whether the fabric manufacturer is responsible, how much it will cost to replace the fabric for customers covered by warranties, and how to account for the cost.

Personal Effectiveness of Finance People

Many people would be technically qualified to work at Herman Miller and perform all the necessary financial functions, but not every finance professional could, or even would want, to work there. At some companies, you would be judged more technically and functionally. Are you a good treasurer or controller? Do your numbers add up? Do you have a good financial strategy? Can you tell us what to do on capital structure? People in financial positions at Herman Miller have to do those things well, but in addition, they have more involvement with people in other functions and more say in company strategy than finance people do in many organizations.

To be successful at Herman Miller, a finance person must be considered to be personally effective. Personal effectiveness requires not only hard skills—the requisite technical skills—but also soft skills such as organizational skills, influencing skills, and interpersonal skills. Max DePree said that efficiency is doing the thing right, and effectiveness is doing the right thing. Leaders can delegate efficiency but must deal personally with effectiveness. Effectiveness comes about through working with others and enabling them to reach their potential.

Soft skills are utilized by people in all functions, including finance, in virtually every aspect of the company's operations—for example, negotiating expense allocation in annual budgeting, making capital budgeting/capital expenditure decisions, and making decisions on adding and allocating capacity.

Balancing Financial Skill Development with Other Demands

Jim Bloem believes that the company's finance people are solid technical citizens and excellent interpersonal relaters. The finance team has a good foundation of technical knowledge and a basic understanding of current financial techniques, but where it can really make a difference is in using those skills in concert with their colleagues in other functions to make good decisions. The finance staff may want to stay generally up to date with technical subjects such as derivatives and the opportunities those products provide, but given the company's relatively straightforward financial structure, doing so must be kept in perspective with other time demands. The company must be adept at foreign exchange exposure management, but rather than trading currency explicitly to make a profit, the finance function focuses mainly on matters such as margins on overseas sales and how adverse currency movements could affect those margins.

Sometimes people within the company must work together as a team to develop new technical knowledge to solve a problem. For example, foreign exchange exposure has increased substantially over the past couple of years, causing the company to reexamine its internal and external exposures. It is the responsibility of the assistant treasurer to develop an exposure identification and management system. If he does not, someone else will have to. But the technical solution he develops to solve the problem is no less important than how he deals with the company's European financial director. They would agree together on the exposures they were hedging, and make a joint decision on what to hedge and how. Translation of subsidiary financial statements is hardly a new topic to the financial director for Europe; he used to be the director of consolidated reporting. This is one of the benefits of the career rotation process. However, now the European financial director has less time for reading financial statements because he is preoccupied with other problems central to the company's European business, such as what price to bid for an important project.

Participative Decision Making

At Herman Miller, no one makes a decision based on rank. The company's decision-making style calls for participation, discussion, and finally, action. The process can be more important than the results of the decision. Decision making requires alignments, working together, arguing a position, and winning only based on the merits of the argument. Inevitably, there are clashes and misunderstandings, unlike more hierarchical organizations where decisions are handed down and conflict is often avoided. But at Herman Miller, how people resolve conflicts is what counts.

The finance function makes only a few types of purely financial decisions independently without involving other functions such as buying or leasing, debt structure, and overall capital structure. Most other kinds of decisions—for example, investment decisions concerning how the company spends money and what it expects in return—are not the province of just the finance function. They are made by larger groups of interested parties.

For executives such as Jim Bloem and Jim Christenson who have worked in other organizations, the participative decision-making process can cause frustrations at first. There is always a shorter way to get there. People who think they know the right answer to a problem must be patient as others come into alignment. But they believe that participative decision making can be a healthy contrast to an atmosphere of confrontation and conflict resolution, where people may worry more about how they are being perceived by others than about the substance of the decision at hand.

Capital Budgeting

The company uses current techniques such as net present value in capital budgeting, but the expected financial return is only one of many factors considered. In companies where Jim Bloem worked before, capital budgeting analysis was done mostly on spreadsheets. When he arrived at Herman Miller, Bloem found an investment decision-making process that was almost completely qualitative. He introduced net present value analysis in order to make the decision-making process more balanced but still participative.

In many companies, capital budgeting decisions are made by a few people at a senior level and handed down. At Herman Miller, the submission and approval process is more participative. Virtually anyone can submit a project for consideration. For example, an administrative person may believe that new word processing equipment is needed. That person writes a memorandum describing the investment required, the cost savings, and all the other reasons the project should be approved. The required format for proposals is relatively flexible; a few calculations are normally included. When the proposal for word processing equipment is considered, the relative merits of this purchase are weighed against others the company may be considering at the same time—for example, new woodworking equipment or a new energy center that is fueled partly by wood scraps from the plant.

If a project is not approved, the person submitting it will always know why. If a project is approved, that person is accountable to other people in the company. If Joe in the plant gets approval for a project, it will not be only because of financial return, but because Joe put his name behind it. If Frank's project is turned down, then Frank will be looking on, making sure Joe lives up to his promises and produces. There is an enforcement and ownership mechanism built into the process.

The finance function does not make the investment decisions, run the process, or act as the enforcer. A finance person would have a difficult time arguing against a new product investment proposal if he or she simply ran the numbers and found that it did not meet the required return. Rather, finance acts as a facilitator, helping the company determine how much it is going to spend. Finance people may assess where the project fits into the strategic plan and provide an independent risk analysis. They may point out items missing or inconsistencies in the proposal. They may observe that research and development is asking for a new product budget that doesn't leave enough funding for new product marketing. They may point out that the design people are excited about a product that marketing does not think will sell. Sometimes, people from other functions invite the finance function to help them resolve a dispute. Finance is able to play this role only if it maintains its impartiality, not taking sides or advocating positions.

Jim Bloem notes that most companies budget the amount they will spend on capital as part of the planning process each year. As a public company, Herman Miller must disclose the amount of its estimated capital spending in its quarterly filings with the Securities and Exchange Commission. At Herman Miller, the sum of all capital budget proposals for the year normally approaches twice the annual capital budget estimated by Bloem and approved by the board just prior to the beginning of each year. Bloem oversees the capital budget proposal winnowing process informally throughout the year in order to ensure that the company stays within its total capital budget as approved and disclosed each year.

Recruiting and Hiring

Herman Miller generally does not hire finance people directly from school. The company is often a finance person's second or third employer. Hiring decisions are made one by one for people with functional expertise to fill specific openings. A good cost accountant may come from the electronics industry, where costs are calculated in fractions of a cent. Resumes from the outside are reviewed. Through the company's job postings, there may be a number of candidates from the inside. Jim Bloem got his job from the inside. He was formerly the company's general counsel, and succeeded Dick Ruch, the former CEO, as CFO.

The ultimate hiring decision is based on who appears most likely to succeed in the effectiveness test, which entails getting things done by working with other people. After accepting the job, it is up to the person to make himself or herself useful, to start developing relationships with people in various functions, and to start forging a career in the company.

Career Ladder

In finance as well as other functions at Herman Miller, career enhancement requires continual development of functional and effectiveness skills. Kermit Campbell, the new CEO, has sent a clear message that he expects people to behave this way.

There are few functional specialists in finance. The cash manager, hired from the outside, is unusual in having done the same job for 11 years. The director of credit management may appear to be a functional specialist, but the job requires a more holistic approach. That person must work with the sales function in making difficult decisions where there is a trade-off between credit risk and sales opportunity.

The career ladder is more horizontal than vertical. It is a process of working in different functions and getting to know the business rather than climbing up in a corporate hierarchy, rung by rung. People become well rounded through job rotation at all levels. The current head of distribution was once the corporate controller. The current corporate controller was once a vice president of marketing and was the controller before that. Finance people are expected to develop both financial and functional competencies. As they rotate through different job assignments, they learn the various disciplines in the finance function such as public accounting, cost accounting, audit, control, credit, and general ledger. They pick up functional skills working with other functions such as design, marketing, manufacturing, or logistics. A person may be hired to fill a finance position in manufacturing. After it becomes known that the person helped reduce the unit cost of a chair by $2.00, someone in logistics may say they have not been able to get a top-quality person to help them organize the routes and automate the shipper selection process.

A move from one finance job to another could be the suggestion of someone like Jim Schreiber, controller, or it could be arranged by the people concerned. A finance person working in operations may discuss trading positions with another person working in market research. The two would consult Schreiber for approval.

Finance people may have stations in the finance area but spend most of their time with the areas to which they are assigned. The finance person assigned to design works mostly at the Design Yard, the company's research center. During a given week that person could be out with a supplier trying to figure out how to get the cost of a component down and hardly be seen by others in finance.

Many jobs are self-defining, and career paths are generally managed by people themselves. The higher the level, the more the boundaries of a job are defined by a person's interests and competencies. For example, directors in the finance function make up their own titles. Their jobs are described as somewhat amoebic in the way they expand and contract with the people filling them. A director's job content is affected by the number of cross-functional teams he or she is invited to join. A director with heavy commitments may ask for more support from below. The CFO and controller oversee this process informally, making sure that there is not excessive overlap in what the directors are doing and that necessary tasks are not being overlooked.

The position of director is a stepping-stone for moving out of the finance function into a general management position. Often, people reach the level of director in their technical accomplishments long before they are awarded the title. The title comes only after there is feedback, mostly informal, from people in the rest of the organization that the individual has helped them achieve their goals.

Organizational Learning

Getting to know the business is equally if not more important than developing financial technical skills. It is impossible to be an effective finance person without knowing the intricacies of the business—how costs are determined, how costs are optimized with design, how suppliers and dealers make money, and how the industry's anachronistic pricing and discount structure works.

What makes the company work is people getting around and talking to each other in the process of getting things done. This fosters organizational learning. Not being a wizard should never be a problem, because the company should be able to get the right people together in a room to solve a problem. Decisions generally are made by groups and not by individuals. Therefore, individual knowledge is important, but collective group knowledge is even more important and powerful.

A person still learning should not be afraid to ask questions, and an experienced person should constantly share his or her knowledge. This takes work because it is human nature to conceal what you don't know. But not being afraid to ask and being willing to tell is a function of trust and self-confidence. It is the essence of organizational learning, and it is at the heart of personal working relationships at Herman Miller.

Performance Evaluation

Finance people are not graded on their technical abilities unless they are deficient. The most important performance criterion is effectiveness, and that hinges on how a person gets things done by working with other people.

In the performance review process, people rate their raters. Casualties include those who are rated poorly from below. The most common complaints are "He didn't train me; he didn't mentor me; he did not participate enough in what I was doing; he didn't help me deal with ambiguity; he didn't help me understand that there are no reporting relationships to utilize in getting this job done, so I had to figure that out for myself." Rarely have people complained about a lack of training in technical areas.

As part of the performance evaluation process, Jim Bloem gives a small written comment on each subsidiary and division controller to each of their bosses. The comments are concerned primarily with technical matters, how they performed the consolidation, whether Bloem was happy with their asset utilization, and a general comment about how well they relate back to the larger organization from his perspective.

Mentoring

Everyone in the company is entitled to mentoring. It works in two directions—being a mentor and having a mentor. Mentoring takes time. Jim Bloem compares it to participating in a seminar. Training comes from sharing. A mentor needs to work on projects with a person to see how that person handles them.

Why People Leave

Finance people seldom leave Herman Miller because they lack the requisite technical skills or because they do not know what their jobs are. Rather, they leave because they are not comfortable dealing with ambiguity—not having clear-cut answers—and having to relate to a variety of other people with different interests to reach a decision. Jim Bloem says that effectiveness on the job does not mean, "Here is my function. Ask me all the right questions. I'll give you all the right answers." Often, new employees are more accustomed to the faster and seemingly more objective decision making found in a more hierarchical organization. Also, in considering why a number of people were unhappy and decided to leave the organization in recent years, Bloem and Chief Counsel Jim Christenson agreed that the reason often boiled down to "not being willing to ask or not wanting to tell."

Scanlon Plan

The company has used a Scanlon Plan since 1949 with the stated intention of making the management process more participative. Under such a plan, a company defines specific goals and employees are paid bonuses based on how well those goals are achieved. Since it was started, Herman Miller's plan has been based on four underlying principles:

- Identity—All employees should understand the business and know how they can be meaningfully involved in meeting its objectives.
- Participation—All employees should work together to accomplish the company's goals and objectives.
- Equity—All employees should realize a fair return on their personal investments of time and talent.
- Competence—All employees should commit their utmost capabilities to the success of the organization.

Today, the Scanlon bonus is an integral part of everyone's compensation. Jim Bloem believes that it gives Herman Miller a competitive advantage, because at many companies people do not understand why they did or did not receive bonuses.

Currently, the amount of the Scanlon bonuses is determined based on four performance criteria:

- Product and service quality. These intangibles are measured by both dealers and customers. If Herman Miller does a good job for the dealer and the dealer does a poor job for the customer, Herman Miller will still get a poor rating from the customer. The customer may give Herman Miller a good grade because the dealer straightened out some of the mistakes the company made, and the dealer's input may hurt the score.
- Asset utilization. The company's goal is two dollars of sales for every dollar of assets; cash is not included in this calculation.
- Growth. This is defined as net income plus net sales divided by two. It is intended to be a measure of both sales and profitability.
- Cost savings suggestions. The amount of savings after the cost of implementation is divided fifty-fifty between the shareholders and the employees

At one point, there were 31 measures, all financial. Examples were days receivable, scrap, and completion percentages. Now the measures are more oriented toward the customer. They include product quality and service quality.

Partnerships with Suppliers and Dealers

Herman Miller makes relatively few components and concentrates rather on designing, assembling, and selling. Suppliers are in effect the company's manufacturers. Pointing to a chair in the conference room, Jim Bloem said that the same supplier had manufactured the internal fiberglass shell for 1,400,000 chairs over a 10-year period.

In establishing a relationship with a supplier, the sourcing function at Herman Miller is concerned with quality, delivery capacity, confidence, and trust. Price is often the last thing discussed. The sourcing function asks three things of suppliers on a continuing basis: be on time, on budget, and on spec.

Pricing is an ongoing issue. Competition in the industry is squeezing margins. Herman Miller is selling for 89 cents today what it sold for a dollar five years ago. A supplier may ask for an increase, and Herman Miller may have to say that the company itself has not had a price increase and cannot afford to increase their component costs. As margins are tightened, a Herman Miller sourcing person may go to a supplier and say that they will have to work together to reduce the cost of a component.

In general, the company tries to establish relationships with suppliers that it does not have to police. However, Herman Miller does like to review the books of its suppliers to see how costs and profits are allocated and what may not be needed. The company tries to maintain a delicate balance, wanting to have trust and not wanting to control the suppliers' profits, but also wanting to make sure that the financial side of the relationship is being run according to the agreed-upon rules.

Margin pressure is also a theme in Herman Miller's dealer relationships. Ten years ago, most sales from dealers were resales. The dealer took title and sold to the end user. Herman Miller was focused primarily on manufacturing and had little contact with the end user. Then, as margins were compressed, dealers could not afford to continue stocking an inventory of finished products for future resale. They could maintain only an inventory of spare parts and a few pieces of furniture to lend to customers in emergencies—for example, when a chair breaks. The dealers continued to have a necessary service function, including design and installation, but had to reduce their asset base to remain profitable.

Now competitive pressure is bringing down order lead times in the industry as well; they have been reduced from as long as 17 weeks to an average of three weeks in the past eight years. Customers worldwide are saying, "If you cannot deliver it in three weeks, I'll get it somewhere else." Like its dealers, Herman Miller cannot afford to keep a large inventory in its Zeeland factory; the company's inventory has actually been reduced by 35 percent in the past two years. The company works with its suppliers to keep the pipeline flowing, but at the same time tries to make only what has been ordered—sometimes a difficult trade-off. This has required Herman Miller to invest in new information systems and arrange EDI (electronic data interchange) with its suppliers. With EDI, business documents such as purchase orders, purchase order acknowledgments, and material release notices can be sent electronically between trade partners. EDI has recently given Herman Miller some competitive advantage, though its lead has been narrowing as EDI has become more widely used in the industry. Improved communication reinforces suppliers and dealers as part of an integral chain and reinforces the covenantal relationships Herman Miller maintains with its external and internal partners.

10

Levi Strauss & Co.

Interview Subjects: *George James, vice chairman and chief financial officer; Joseph M. Maurer, vice president and treasurer; Richard D. Murphy, vice president and controller; Katherine Woodall, senior manager, Corporate Communications*

Executive Summary

Levi Strauss & Co. (LS&CO.) is a company driven by values. No CEO has made a stronger statement than LS&CO. Chairman and CEO Robert Haas about the importance of values in guiding everyone in the company. LS&CO.'s management defined its values in the Aspirations Statement at a critical time, shortly after undertaking a leveraged buy-out, when requirements to stay competitive in the apparel industry were changing and some thought the famous jeans maker was losing its focus. It defined six values in its Aspirations Statement: new behaviors, diversity, recognition, ethical management practices, communications, and empowerment. In defining those values, LS&CO. set the stage for a new style of management in which decisions would be made by people closest to the product and the customer. Now, management's job is to set parameters and negotiate goals with people. The Aspirations Statement guides how LS&CO. works with all of its partners, including employee/owners, vendors, retailers, and financial institutions.

The role of the finance function in this cultural change has been to become more integrated with the marketing and manufacturing side of the business, to be less expert oriented and more team oriented, to help people in business units do their jobs more efficiently and effectively, and to help business managers understand the link between strategic business plans and return-on-investment targets. Now there are fewer technical specialists in the finance function and more people who move from finance to operating assignments. The finance function is working with human resources to design an incentive-based compensation program called Partners in Performance that links each person's compensation to shareholder value. LS&CO.'s management believes that maintaining superior financial performance and keeping shareholders happy will earn it the privilege of preserving its values-oriented culture.

Background

Levi Strauss & Co. was founded in 1850 during the Gold Rush in California by a Bavarian immigrant named Levi Strauss. The company sold denim work pants that became known as blue jeans. Levi's® has remained the best-known brand name in jeans since then. Today, the company has sales of close to $6 billion and employs more than 36,000 people.

Because of the almost universal popularity of jeans among young people, the company enjoyed a period of steady growth and prosperity during the postwar period until the late 1970s. At that time, growth in the total market for jeans began to level, and the company started to diversify into related apparel, leveraging the strength of its brand name. Though related apparel such as denim shirts and Dockers® casual apparel have recently been quite successful, the first attempts to put the Levi's® name on other types of apparel were not all profitable. Some analysts at the time thought the company was beginning to lose focus.

Robert Haas, the great great grandnephew of Levi Strauss, became CEO in 1984 at age 43. The company was taken private in an LBO in 1985. Haas faced the dual challenge of restoring the company's growth and profitability and servicing the heavy debt of an LBO. In an interview with editor Robert Howard published in the September–October 1990 issue of the *Harvard Business Review,* Haas described coming to grips with the company's values, listening to suppliers, customers, and employees, and redefining the strategy of the company.

Values Drive the Company

Haas had always heard people talk about the "soft stuff" and the "hard stuff." The soft stuff was a company's commitment to its workforce. The hard stuff was what really mattered—getting the pants out the door. Now he saw they were becoming intertwined. He said, "A company's values—what it stands for, what its people believe in—are crucial to its competitive success. Indeed, values drive the business."

Haas explains that in earlier years, businesses like LS&CO. were less affected by changing market forces, and boundaries were clearer. Geographic boundaries defined markets, and there were clear distinctions among suppliers, customers, workers, and managers. LS&CO. sold to a fragmented domestic market of some 10,000 accounts. People's work expectations were different then. They gave their loyalty in exchange for job security and benefits. In this environment, typical of American companies during most of the postwar period, a command-and-control style of management was the norm.

By the late 1980s, the environment had changed. Markets had become more competitive with fewer geographic barriers. Improved information technology had allowed consumer tastes and products to change more quickly. Fifty large customers accounted for more than half of LS&CO.'s domestic business. People had become more mobile, partly because corporate restructuring and downsizing forced them to look for new jobs. A slow-moving hierarchical organization that made decisions at the top was not suited to this new marketplace.

Flatter Organization

While taking the painful step of reducing the company's total workforce by one-third, Haas created a flatter organization with the objective of empowering people closest to the product and the customer. People could no longer be supervised as they had been in the past; decisions had to be made too fast. People had to be guided by strategy and values. Management's job was to set parameters, to negotiate goals with people, to encourage them to take initiative, and to be accountable for their decisions. There were fewer layers of management and less review. Now Treasurer Joe Maurer explains, "If there's no value added, there's no review."

Haas believes that organizations often encourage people to protect their turf and be political, but that people's ideals are often different. Part of management's job is to liberate them so they can act out those ideals.

LS&CO.'s management carefully thought out the company's ideals and values in 1987 and summarized them in the Aspirations Statement (figure 18).

FIGURE 18: Aspirations Statement

We all want a company that our people are proud of and committed to, where all employees have an opportunity to contribute, learn, grow, and advance based on merit, not politics or background. We want our people to feel respected, treated fairly, listened to, and involved. Above all, we want satisfaction from accomplishments and friendships, balanced personal and professional lives, and to have fun in our endeavors.

When we describe the kind of LS&CO. we want in the future, what we are talking about is building on the foundation we have inherited: affirming the best in our company's traditions, closing gaps that may exist between principles and practices, and updating some of our values to reflect contemporary circumstances.

What type of leadership is necessary to make our Aspirations a reality?

New behaviors: Leadership that exemplifies directness, openness to influence, commitment to the success of others, willingness to acknowledge our own contributions to problems, personal accountability, teamwork, and trust. Not only must we model these behaviors but we must coach others to adopt them.

Diversity: Leadership that values a diverse workforce (age, sex, ethnic group, etc.) at all levels of the organization, diversity in experience, and diversity in perspectives. We have committed to taking full advantage of the rich backgrounds and abilities of all our people and to promoting a greater diversity in positions of influence. Differing points of view will be sought; diversity will be valued and honesty rewarded, not suppressed.

Recognition: Leadership that provides greater recognition—both financial and psychic—for individuals and teams that contribute to our success. Recognition must be given to all who contribute: those who create and innovate and also those who continually support the day-to-day business requirements.

Ethical management practices: Leadership that epitomizes the stated standards of ethical behavior. We must provide clarity about our expectations and must enforce these standards through the corporation.

Communications: Leadership that is clear about company, unit, and individual goals and performance. People must know what is expected of them and receive timely, honest feedback on their performance and career aspirations.

Empowerment: Leadership that increases the authority and responsibility of those closest to our products and customers. By actively pushing responsibility, trust, and recognition into the organization, we can harness and release the capabilities of all our people.

Values and Strategic Planning

The company is spending millions of dollars up front in leadership training programs, expecting a payoff over the long term. All functions of the company attend the seminars. People at different levels from different functions attend together. The top 200 managers in the company participate in teaching the seminars. George James, CFO, teaches two each year. The senior management faculty both teach and participate. Their leadership ability is tested as they interact and become indistinguishable members of the group. By interacting and maintaining their leadership positions, they try to demonstrate what it takes to meet the company's Aspirations.

Importance of Values in the Finance Function

CFO George James finds it hard to say that any one of the company's values is more important than any of the others. They are all important and all interrelated. But he says that ethics stand out. Empowering people must be done in an ethical framework; otherwise people do not trust each other or feel they have the authority and responsibility to act.

Treasurer Joe Maurer points in particular to diversity. The more truly diverse the people who work for LS&CO. in areas such as culture and personality, the more the company will reflect society. LS&CO.'s products are destined for all of society, not just for a particular target group. By being truly diverse, LS&CO. can recruit the best people and bring out the best in the people working for the company.

Controller Rick Murphy points to empowerment and communication. He recalls that when people started talking to each other, things started falling into place. As the company implemented its Aspirations, people were so diligent in keeping each other informed that "you already told me that" became an in-house joke.

Employee Partnerships

Murphy believes that the spirit of teamwork pervades the organization and affects the way people feel and work. He contrasts the atmosphere at LS&CO. with public accounting and other large corporations in which people behave and do things "in a certain way." The requirement for top-caliber people to work their hardest is evident here as in every successful large corporation, but at the same time, there is a casual, friendly atmosphere with flexible working hours and an informal dress code. The ability to wear Levi's® and Dockers® products to work is one of the company's most popular benefits! Professionals are encouraged to take risks and not to be afraid to fail—and learn in the process. This feeling extends into the manufacturing plants. One employee commented, "We no longer have to check our brains at the door."

LS&CO. was recently cited for having one of the highest proportions of minorities in management of any U.S. corporation in a book by Lawrence Otis Graham, *The Best Companies for Minorities.* It was one of the 10 corporations given an Optimas Award by *Personnel Journal* in 1992 for the performance of its human resource function. In all 10 of the companies that won the award, the human resources function is a participant in the corporate decision-making process, human resource policies are integrated with overall strategic planning, human resource programs are consistent with overall business goals, and human resource programs are considered cost-effective. *Personnel Journal* cited four human resources initiatives that Donna Goya, LS&CO.'s senior vice president of human resources, considers to have particular priority. They are (1) the CORE Curriculum, a training program that includes leadership, ethics, and diversity; (2) Total Remuneration, also known within the company as REM 2000, a compensation plan being designed to keep the company competitive into the next century; (3) health and safety; and (4) a work/family balance. Each of the human resources function's initiatives is meant to support three key strategies: (1) to align all human resource programs and policies with the Aspirations Statement; (2) to develop human resource systems that will instill continuous improvement in the company's business systems, work processes, and employees; and (3) to promote the health, safety, and well-being of all employees.

Business Partnerships

Haas describes LS&CO. as a marketer rather than a manufacturer at the center of a seamless web of mutual responsibility and collaboration. LS&CO.'s objective is to manage the entire chain from the fabric manufacturer to the retailer as an integrated business. It is in LS&CO.'s best interest for its partners to be prosperous. The company reduced its U.S. denim suppliers from 10 or 12 to 4 or 5 larger, closer relationships. It established LeviLink™, a pioneering data interchange system that allows retailers to update their inventories by size and style and order replenishments electronically. LS&CO. sales representatives now help retailers analyze store sales data and display and sell company products more effectively.

Conformance to values is an important issue for all of LS&CO.'s business partners, including suppliers, retailers, and financial institutions. Environmental policies are particularly important. CFO George James chairs an environmental task force that sets standards for contractors around the world. Compliance with regulations and LS&CO.'s own standards in categories such as water pollution is part of the company's terms of engagement with its contractors.

Information sharing between business partners is also important. Treasurer Joe Maurer cites LS&CO.'s long-standing handshake relationship with its supplier Cone Mills. When that company was planning a public offering that would put a substantially larger portion of its stock in public hands, it approached LS&CO. to discuss possible concerns over a change in control. The spirit of the conversation was, "What makes sense for both of us? What do you need and what do we need?"

Financial Institution Partnerships

Maurer describes relationships with the outside financial community not as adversarial, but rather as based on partnerships. The company's preferred method for dealing with financial institutions is to sit on the same side of the table and share the same information. If a bank differed from LS&CO. on a core values issue, the relationship would most likely be terminated. LS&CO.'s principal banks have been with them since the LBO. The company plans to maintain a relatively small number of substantial, profitable banking relationships. For the majority of banks, LS&CO. has no business to offer, and in line with the Aspirations Statement, Joe Maurer considers it only fair to communicate that clearly.

LS&CO. does not expect pricing concessions from its banks, but neither does it expect to pay a premium. It is open in sharing financial information with its banks. Both the company and the banks believe that negative surprises are not appropriate. When a bank comes to LS&CO. with a proprietary financial product, the company does not shop the idea around. There is mutual trust.

Finance People as Business Partners

George James has helped extend the company's informal atmosphere into the finance function, creating what Joe Maurer describes as a collegial spirit. The finance function is becoming more team oriented and less expert oriented. Rather than working and sharing ideas primarily among themselves, finance professionals often join business units and regularly work in cross-functional teams. Their mission is to learn the business, to help people in the business units do their jobs more efficiently and effectively, and to add value to the enterprise in whatever ways they can. They are trying to make their analysis more meaningful to business people without a financial background and to help business managers understand the link between strategic business plans and return-on-investment (ROI) targets.

James described an annual conference of key financial people in which the stated agenda was technical subjects—cost accounting, taxes, the Financial Accounting Standards Board, etc. The real agenda turned out to be teamwork—teams within treasury, teams across different groups in the finance function, and cross-functional teams.

Finance People in Working Groups

Finance people are now involved in cross-functional teams with a wide variety of missions. Currently, 48 groups are active. Each group has a senior management sponsor. When a member of management is asked by a new group to be a sponsor, the manager makes sure that the group's activities will be coordinated with and will not overlap the activities of other groups currently active.

Examples of groups include the following:

- The Global Environmental Council assesses and sets global environmental policies.
- The Indoor Air Quality Task Force assesses air quality and determines necessary building modifications.
- The Business Resumption Steering Committee develops contingency plans for all mission critical business processes and departments.
- The 501® Global Task Force coordinates marketing strategy for the Levi's 501® brand worldwide. It deals with issues such as counterfeiting and arbitrage caused by cross-border price discrepancies.
- The 501 Keeper of the Keys Group works to make the Levi's 501® product consistent on a global basis.
- The Global Networking Forum is concerned with information needs and communication throughout the company's global network.
- The Capital Expenditure Working Committee is concerned with procedures for submission and approval of capital expenditures.
- The Capital Structure and Liquidity Group is concerned with the company's capital structure and the ongoing liquidity needs of all the company's functions.

Finance people help to determine the cost and other financial impacts of the groups' missions. For example, in the Business Resumption Steering Committee, finance people helped determine the $12 to $15 million daily impact if the company were unable to function, the cost of contingency measures, and ways to maintain necessary controls in the event of a disaster such as an earthquake or a fire.

Sometimes ad hoc groups are assembled within these task forces to solve specific problems. For example, finance people in the 501 Global Task Force played a key role in developing a solution to a problem caused by a large difference in prices for Levi's 501s® between the United States and Europe. Unauthorized intermediaries were buying 501s in the United States and selling them in Europe, undercutting the company's European customers. The pricing discrepancy arose because of the different way Levi's® jeans are perceived in the two markets. In the United States, Levi's® originated as and have always been reasonably priced work pants, though they are considered fashionable as well. In Europe, they were considered fashion items right from the beginning, and therefore priced higher than most work pants in that market.

Part of the finance function's mission in the Capital Expenditure Working Committee and the Capital Structure and Liquidity Group is to ensure that needs of other functions are being served on a continuing basis.

Controller Rick Murphy recounts that when the company started to put together cross-functional teams, there were "woodwork people" who had been with the company forever, knew its systems backwards and forwards, and didn't talk to anybody. Their attitude was, "Here's my job; I know how to do it. I won't answer any questions because I know the answers anyway." They were not introverted, just used to the old way of doing things and "categorized into their jobs." When they first came to team meetings they would not say anything. After some time, one might remark, "Alex knows how to do it," or, "I'll tell you how to do it, but I'm not doing the work." Gradually, they came out of their "silos." They became more excited about team endeavors and more helpful.

Finance People Working with Business Managers

Finance people are helping business managers with their strategic plans and annual plans and helping them interpret their financial results. LS&CO. is trying to develop a model of a finance person who does not just provide accounting data to operating people, but also helps with analysis of what the information means. In the past, a finance person might have said that inventory was too high. Today, that person's job is to say why it is too high and recommend what can be done about it. Finance people are working with operating people to analyze product line and customer profitability. Before the LBO, the Levi's® brand was so profitable that there was little incentive to analyze the profitability of any of its segments.

Working with business managers requires learning the business. Finance people are learning the business by reading, by traveling to get familiar with manufacturing and retail operations, and by participating in task forces to address business problems.

Finance People Assigned to Brands

LS&CO.'s domestic business has recently been reorganized along brand lines, rather than marketing divisions as it was in the past. A large number of the corporate finance staff—about 300 people—are being assigned to North America over the next 18 months. People closer to the brands will be more oriented to analysis and decision making than accounting. They will be supported by smaller, specialized corporate staffs in the headquarters office. The core accounting staff will act as a service function for the brands, while the corporate finance function will provide strategic support.

This reorganization puts finance people closer to where decisions are made; decisions can be made jointly by operations and finance people. When operating managers actually pay the finance person's salary, they have more confidence in that person; he or she is one of them. Finance people can help brand managers analyze inventory turnover, calculate product line and customer profitability, and optimize the product mix. They can help business managers develop the best customer service methods. They can look for the best ways to measure performance.

Teams to Support Largest Customers

LS&CO. has noticed a growing concentration in its largest retail accounts. The company is planning to create teams to deal with its 50 most important customers, perhaps located near those customers. Finance people on the teams will focus on matters such as inventory turnover, account profitability, and the customers' financials and credit risk to LS&CO. Finance people will work with line people on customer relations. It is in LS&CO.'s best interest to help its customers be profitable and identify areas of further efficiency.

Account profitability studies will include the costs to service each account. With that information, the sales function can consider alternative ways to service accounts or possible changes in the mix—for example, advertising versus in-store promotion. LS&CO. wants first to agree with a customer on what the company will do, what it will provide, and when, and then execute the agreement as close as possible to 100 percent of the time. The company is developing measures of its own performance in meeting that objective.

Overseas Sourcing: Hard and Soft Costs

Rick Murphy describes how one of the finance operations teams has raised awareness for sourcing decisions in a new way, taking both hard and soft costs into account. Products generally were sourced from whatever place provided the lowest cost. Nearby contractors were considered to save transportation costs, and then the one with the best price/quantity ratio was selected. As the company grew, it started sourcing in other parts of the world. Standard costs were reduced but quality deteriorated. The sourcing process became more complicated. People had to make long trips to select, negotiate with, and manage vendors. Sometimes it seemed to take forever to get the product.

True costs, as the team described them, included soft costs such as lead time, cancellations, markdowns, lateness, and merchandising trips. Hard costs were based on accounting rules. Soft costs were based on estimates that everyone concerned agreed on. For example, the team estimated that one day's delay cost $.007 per unit. Sourcing decisions were reevaluated, and this provided an important example of teamwork between finance and operations people to achieve the company's goals.

Finance people are part of a reengineering process that will reduce lead times and inventories to calculate profitability and to identify other possible trade-offs.

Financial Model for Plant Clusters

Since 1850, in Murphy's words, the company has expanded by personality. Plants were located where the people in charge wanted them to be. Recently, a wider group including the finance function looked at the manufacturing process to see if there is a way to get the product to the customer sooner and at less expense. Generally, the group concluded that plants should be located where the company sells most of its product and that functions such as manufacturing, finishing, and distribution should be located together in plant clusters. The finance function helped develop a model in concert with the company's reengineering process that showed the investment the company would have to make to move people and equipment to create plant clusters. The model helps determine an optimum product mix within a cluster and allocate the manufacturing of a given product among different locations.

Improved Standard Costing

Murphy sees finance and planning people working for brand managers becoming more "part of the fabric." In the old days, "debit and credit people" would wait for paperwork from the field to prove entries and calculate standard costs. Because of timing, fabric price, and other differences, the standard costs they calculated usually did not match after-the-fact standard costs. Now finance people are getting out of their offices and into the business, analyzing all the costs, seeing the reasons for all the variances, and learning the design of the business. Now their entries on the ledger result as much from what they learn inside the divisions as from numbers in reports they receive in the mail.

Empowering the Finance Function

For Murphy, empowerment means whatever it takes to help a person do his or her job. There must be both hard and soft controls. On the hard side, policies and procedures are required. On the soft side, there are people. Finance people have to lighten up to help overcome the skepticism of operating people, and operating people have to put aside their stereotypes of finance people. It must be explained that control extends throughout the company and that it is for everyone's betterment. People must understand the reasons for rules, how control works, and how it can help them. They must see control as a positive force, not a negative force and not against human values. The way finance people can win their argument is to show that control does not have to do with any personal, departmental, or divisional gain, but that good controls benefit the company as a whole.

Changing the Philosophy of Internal Audit

CFO George James points out that there is a lot of compliance in finance—rules and procedures that must be followed to the letter. Internal audit, a function with an independent role to ensure that the company has proper controls, can cause friction between empowerment and people trying to carry out their responsibility in the correct way. The company has tried to change the philosophy of the internal audit. Traditionally, the auditor has been a watchdog, coming up with a list of everything that is wrong. Now the auditors will sit down with the manager of a group, explain why they are there, why the audit needs to be done, and how it will help them attain the goals of the business. Perhaps the auditors will ask if there are things they should be looking at that might help the manager. After the audit has been completed, the CFO asks the business manager for a report on how well the auditors did their job, and whether they carried out their role in a supportive way. The manager being audited reviews the auditors' report before anyone else sees it. The report is sent up the chain only if there are real problems, such as a severe lack of control in some area. Now that managers see the auditors acting in a more supportive way, they have started to ask auditors to help with special projects. The auditors' role is still to make sure controls are in place, but now what matters is how they go about it.

Bringing External Auditors on Board

When the company began to change its management style, the external auditors were a little uncomfortable, but they could not describe exactly why. In deciding how they were going to audit the company, they relied on what they knew to be a solid control base and used the criterion of materiality as a safety net in determining what they were going to check out in detail. They might not have felt they could take the same approach in a smaller company. They relied more on talking to people and getting a feel for what was going on than they had in the past. Murphy comments, "We even got them into our casual clothing!"

Treasury an Empowered Function

Treasurer Joe Maurer considers treasury itself to be an empowered function that operates within established guidelines and shared objectives. This is possible because there is a clear understanding of the company's tolerance for financial risk. However, in some functions within treasury, such as foreign exchange and debt management, there are tight controls and very few people are authorized to execute transactions. It is empowerment with clear limits. Foreign exchange, for example, is a specialized function. Because of its international structure, the company chooses to manage it centrally. Business with financial institutions is concentrated and tightly controlled to give the company maximum leverage in negotiating pricing.

Cost/Benefit of Controls

While persuading operating people to consider the benefit of controls, the finance function has also tried to see which controls may no longer be necessary or cost-effective. The credit function used to order a Dun & Bradstreet report on each new vendor to guard against selling to bogus vendors. When it was determined that no false vendors had been detected by the procedure, the requirement was changed.

Information Sharing

If someone is looking for information within the company, not many questions are asked about the need to know. It is generally known whether the person has a need to know or they would not be asking for the information. The finance function has facilitated sharing a lot of information among operating units in the company. If there is a problem with Dockers® products in the United States, the managers in

Australia will know about it. George James believes that a centralized database of information is an important way to empower employees but admits that LS&CO. is not there yet.

The company has four town meetings and an annual meeting each year for all shareholders to review the business. A financial report is always on the agenda. Levi Strauss & Co. is required to file as much financial information as any public company. There is an open forum for questions that gives management an idea of the information people want.

Consensus Decision Making

Treasurer Joe Maurer believes that it is easy for an experienced finance professional to feel he or she knows exactly what to do, and to want to do it without waiting to discuss it and explain it. Indeed, there are times when the treasury function has no choice but to act expeditiously. The toughest part is slowing down the process, bringing everybody else on board, saying, "Here is what we need to do," and asking, "What do you think?" The more important the decision, the more important it is to share information and gain a consensus before moving forward.

Recruiting for Finance Professionals

In addition to intelligence, flexibility, experience, and diversity, LS&CO. looks for people who can have a real impact on the business and a positive influence on the culture. Maurer looks for people who are "broad enough to see the big picture" and "able to hit the ground running." He looks for the kind of people who will interact well with other divisions and who have the skills to work in other areas of the company and perhaps the ability to someday become general managers. He believes that these standards are not hard to find because LS&CO. sees the best available people in its management recruiting. Candidates are expected to know a lot about the company, including the Aspirations Statement, and they do. They tend to have not only good technical skills but also a strong commitment to values, as evidenced by activities such as community service.

The finance function has recently been hiring six or seven MBA students during the summers even when there are no permanent job openings. It helps get the word around about who LS&CO. is, what it is like to work there, and what the Aspirations are. One summer intern from the Darden Business School at the University of Virginia had worked as an analyst at Morgan Stanley before business school. He managed a financing for LS&CO. in Hungary that turned out to be the country's second-ever public bond offering.

Spherical Performance Evaluation

During the annual planning process, the CFO agrees with his immediate subordinates on four or five key objectives that will be used for performance evaluation at the end of the year. He also has a checklist of Aspirational behavior. The controller and treasurer go through a similar process with their direct reports. In doing a performance evaluation, a supervisor consults a "spherical group" of peers and operating people the person works with. In evaluating the controller and treasurer, the CFO may talk to 9 or 10 people. A person is asked for three positive and three negative observations concerning the person being evaluated. The negatives are used as coaching points in describing to a person how he or she is seen. People skills are always the hardest issue to deal with; technical skills are not as hard to evaluate.

Finance Career Paths

The company wants to hire people with broad capabilities and develop them internally so that they have the flexibility either to advance in the finance function or to move into line functions and take on general management responsibilities. LS&CO. is a marketing company, and people need direct line experience to move ahead. Finance people will have that opportunity more and more, but George James says that the key is to get them involved early enough that they can develop well-rounded careers. If a person starts with the company in treasury and then moves to planning, his or her next assignment should be on the operating side. LS&CO. wants people who have credibility in understanding the chain. It is beginning to work. The company's general manager in the Czech Republic has a background in the controller's function. Recently, a finance person was selected as a national sales manager, and finance people were selected to fill two divisional controllers' positions more on the basis of interpersonal skills and overall knowledge of the business than technical skills. There hasn't yet been much crossover the other way—back into finance—but that may happen more in the future as part of a management development plan.

Compensation Based on Shareholder Value

The REM 2000 Task Force has looked at the way business unit performance is measured and at the whole spectrum of remuneration, including cash, benefits, performance-based bonuses, psychic income, and everything else an employee gets for working at LS&CO. The result has been a "pay-for-performance" program based on contribution to shareholder value. With the help of the human resource and finance functions, management has invested a great deal of time in getting people from all functions to understand why shareholder value is important and how team cooperation creates it.

The Partners in Performance Program, starting in 1995, will affect the annual and long-term planning process. For some time, LS&CO. has had an incentive plan under which managers have been paid for performance against plan. But now the entire company, including the finance function, is changing the way both performance and plan are calculated by emphasizing return on investment. Managers will now have to think about the balance sheet as well as the income statement. They will be paid based on how they create shareholder value. For the company as a whole, the calculation of shareholder value will be based on company performance, measured by the three-year increase in stock price plus dividends compared to the Standard & Poor's 400. The resulting shareholder value will then be adjusted for each division and individual based on their contribution to overall results. A business manager might be measured based on the value of his or her business as if it were independent, and people at all levels of that business might be measured on how they contributed to its overall goal. This practice is making everyone think more externally. The merchandising person is not just supporting a sales person within the company but helping the sales person deal with the retailer.

In the past, managers submitted operating plans that tended to be conservative and easy to exceed. Now it will be assumed that managers know their businesses and what is possible. They will be challenged to think about the best they can do. Rather than submitting a single plan, each manager will be asked to develop several alternative scenarios based on different assumptions. Senior management will discuss the different options with the business managers and then agree on the final plans.

Managers will have some latitude in how they meet their objectives. Some managers may reach their goals by actually shrinking their businesses to improve returns. There will be an annual target. The manager will be paid a bonus if the target is exceeded. The target may not be the same as the annual plan. It will be set by the manager and the finance function. Bonuses will be paid based on shareholder value. This will align what management is doing with the ultimate payout to the shareholders—increased share value.

Joe Maurer explains that the company's motivation for building shareholder value is not just financial; it is deeper. The company must earn the privilege of preserving its culture through superior performance. By being economically efficient and showing good financial performance in comparison with other companies, the company will satisfy the needs of the shareholders. In this way, the company will be able to preserve the kind of culture it wants, with its values, commitment to the community, and everything else it stands for.

11

Silicon Graphics, Inc.

Interview Subject: *Stanley J. Meresman, senior vice president, finance, and chief financial officer*

Executive Summary

Silicon Graphics, Inc. (SGI) is a story of managing growth and change. Founded just 12 years ago, the company has about $1.5 billion in sales and employs about 4,200 people in 80 locations worldwide. Many of the founders, who came largely from Stanford, are still at the company. The CEO of 10 years, Ed McCracken, preserves the entrepreneurial spirit of the early years while managing a 35 percent annual growth rate in an industry undergoing rapid change.

SGI's culture encourages finance people to be hands on, to initiate, to take risks, but to flag problems as soon as they are identified. The company considers itself apolitical. Using position power or taking personal credit for team efforts is met with the response, "We don't do that here."

The finance function at SGI is largely decentralized and matrix managed. Activities such as cost accounting for the manufacturing organization and profitability analysis for the divisions are decentralized because line managers consider them to add value. General managers view division controllers as business partners and critical members of their teams. Division controllers and other finance staff members report straight line to division managers and dotted line to the parent corporate controller. However, when a finance person using best judgment says "no" to a division manager, the CFO and the corporate controller will support that decision.

Background

SGI is the leading supplier of high-performance visual computer systems. The company was founded to pioneer three-dimensional computing. Today, SGI's systems allow users to create true-color, three-dimensional environments on the screen, move objects, change the viewer's perspective, and simulate a variety of conditions. SGI's equipment has become a necessary tool for sophisticated users such as airplane and automobile manufacturers, architects, intelligence agencies, pharmaceutical companies, and film makers who use animation, special effects, or simulated environments, products, or physics.

For example, SGI equipment was used to generate the underwater scenes in *Hunt for Red October* and many of the special effects scenes for *Jurassic Park, Death Becomes Her, Terminator 2,* and *Beauty and the Beast.* All the leading animators who work for directors like Steven Spielberg or George Lucas use SGI systems. In aircraft repair, a maintenance person points the mouse at the part of the plane displayed on the computer screen and sees the appropriate instruction. He or she sees how things work in a three-dimensional picture that can be moved about and hears audio comments from a maintenance engineer. In the automobile industry, SGI computer graphics have largely replaced drawings, clay models, and wood models. A new car can be designed and visualized in three dimensions, with different colors and fabrics and under different lighting conditions. Stress on the engine, wheels, and other parts of the car can be simulated. An architect can, in effect, walk through a model of a house, see the sunlight at various times of day, and perhaps decide to change the angle of the house on the lot or the location of the windows before the house is built.

In June 1992, SGI acquired MIPS Computer Systems, Inc., a leader in RISC processor technology. Renamed MIPS Technologies, Inc., it operates as a wholly owned subsidiary and continues to proliferate the MIPS RISC architecture into the computer and consumer electronics industries. (RISC stands for reduced instruction set computing.)

Company Values

The company's values were instilled by McCracken and the founders at the beginning. Stan Meresman, CFO, interprets SGI's current values as follows:

Principles—Working with Other People

- ☐ Respect people, their differences, and their diversity.
- ☐ Treat people with dignity.
- ☐ Listen to people; seek their input.
- ☐ Communicate to people so that they understand what we're trying to do.
- ☐ Empower people.
- ☐ Be demanding but tolerant.
- ☐ Do the right thing.
- ☐ Be part of the solution rather than part of the problem.

Values—Working within the Company Culture

- ☐ Be hands on.
- ☐ Make it happen; show a "can-do" attitude.
- ☐ Be proactive, initiate, take a risk.
- ☐ Go for it.
- ☐ Make a difference.
- ☐ Be a leader.
- ☐ Be flexible, open to opportunities.
- ☐ Subject what you are thinking of doing to the TV test. You should be willing to explain it on TV or to your employees and not feel embarrassed.
- ☐ Hold people accountable for results and give them visibility.
- ☐ Flag problems early.
- ☐ Reward results, not effort.

Values—Description of Company Culture

- ☐ People are our most important assets.
- ☐ We have an open-door policy.
- ☐ People make a big contribution to all the things we do.
- ☐ Everybody is a worker.
- ☐ There is a diversity of ways to go about things.
- ☐ There is no single, best, right answer.
- ☐ SGI is not a political company; it deemphasizes position power.
- ☐ Results and accountability are essential.
- ☐ This is an environment where you are encouraged to take risks; mistakes happen, but you are expected to learn from them.
- ☐ Own your own job, your performance, your career, and your development.

SGI's values are described more formally in the Spirit of SGI (figure 19).

FIGURE 19: The Spirit of SGI

We who...

are open and receptive, hear and understand
talk straight and honest, are heard and understood.

We who...

are full of enthusiasm and fun, watch it spill over and catch on,
respect, trust and support, are lifted above our squabbles.

We who...

seek solutions rather than blame, fuel and sustain our growth
empower others and delegate, find our scope increased.

We who...

set objectives and propagate them, find our objectives met
encourage creativity, see results beyond our expectations.

CEO Values

Ed McCracken, the CEO for the past 10 years, is concerned about not "losing the edge." He believes that companies in this business need to keep taking risks, encouraging—indeed pushing—their people to make bold bets that are inherently risky, and to reward and celebrate successes so that their people will feel like winners. SGI must continue to be a "go-for-it" company and not act conservative like a typical big, successful company. It cannot be complacent or arrogant. It is only as good as the last product introduced and last quarter's results. One of the reasons for keeping MIPS Technologies, Inc., separate from SGI was to preserve that entrepreneurial spirit prevalent in a smaller entity.

Anticipating and Producing Change

CFO Stan Meresman explains that the company views change as an opportunity. Companies that don't change and reorganize to keep up with the rapid evolution in their marketplaces will end up declining. He points to the recent troubles at IBM and Digital. The key to achieving competitive advantage is not just reacting to change, but in producing change. To be successful at the $5 billion dollar sales level, SGI will need to be doing things differently than it is today at the $1.5 billion dollar level, even though what is being done today is successful. SGI needs to anticipate what will be required in order to be successful down the road and begin to work to be sure it is in place before needed. "If it ain't broke, don't fix it" is a philosophy that has no application here—constant improvement is what the company is all about.

Apolitical Company

Stan Meresman believes that SGI is largely successful at remaining an apolitical company. A personal or hidden agenda is considered unacceptable. Everything should be discussed openly and "on the table." Claiming personal credit for a team effort or making derogatory remarks to hurt a colleague draws the response, "We don't do that here." People at SGI have a healthy respect for one another.

Speaking Up

In SGI's culture, if you see something that does not look right, you should do something about it, even if that requires getting "in someone's face" outside your area of responsibility. You can talk to your manager, supervisor, or vice president, the CFO, or even the president, whoever you feel comfortable with. If it's not right, don't tolerate it, but communicate. Be proud of your company. Identify with it. It may turn out that it *is* right and you just didn't understand the reasons, or maybe it isn't right and management was oblivious to it.

Risk Taking

In the SGI environment, it is safe to take a risk, and it's acceptable to fail—once in a while, as long as you learn from it. Occasional failure is consistent with taking risks. When the inevitable problem occurs, the appropriate response is to fix it, to think about the process, and to think about how to prevent this and similar problems from happening again. What's not acceptable is making a mistake and disguising or concealing the problem while trying to solve it on your own.

Giving a "Heads Up"

When a potential problem is looming, it is important in the SGI culture to give a "heads up" as soon as possible. Voice mail is used for even the most sensitive messages. What counts is getting the message quickly to the person who needs it.

How this works can be illustrated with an example. Last year, the vice president of marketing took responsibility for all the company's trade show equipment. His staff did a physical count for the first time in six months and estimated that they were $200,000 to $400,000 short. They had no idea where the equipment was because it had been shipped back and forth to many trade shows in the past six months. They had not recorded the serial numbers. The missing equipment might have sat inside SGI's loading docks for weeks because nobody was looking for it, or it might have been put in some other division's inventory. The vice president immediately flagged the problem, informing the CFO and others with a "heads up" voice mail. He and his accountant developed a new inventory tracking system. They developed a plan to reduce the department's discretionary expenses by about $200,000 for the coming quarter, and they were able to meet that plan. Unfortunately, the shortage turned out to be in the upper range of their estimate, but the financial impact was partially mitigated by their quick expense-reduction initiative. They were not defensive, and they did not say that they inherited the problem from someone else. They simply explained what the situation was, what they were doing about it, and how they were going to prevent it from happening again. Given the problem, this was good behavior within the SGI culture.

Empowerment

Stan Meresman describes empowerment as critical to an organization that is committed to change. Management spends its time describing the vision and the overall direction, aligning people, and letting them "go for it."

There are many different ways to do everything. All of the acceptable ways to solve a problem could be envisioned as falling within a box, or solution window. Getting the answer anywhere in that box is just fine. Different people will end up in different places in the box, approaching problems in their own ways. If you do a pulse check and find they are heading in a different direction and there's no way they are going to hit the box, you need to get them realigned. You trust people to do the right thing, to figure out how to do it their own way in order to get within the solution window, and you just let them go for it.

This attitude allows for tremendous diversity, not only in people's backgrounds but also in ways of approaching things. The company fosters a diversity of approaches and styles. People are encouraged to think independently with the overall goals in mind.

Meresman contrasts SGI's environment to that of some other companies, where the CEO may believe that there is one right way to do something and that systems are needed to watch for people who don't do it the right way. This type of micromanagement just breaks down when an organization reaches a certain size. A company such as SGI needs the ability to change quickly. An organization of empowered teams is able to provide the necessary flexibility and foster enthusiasm and drive. Protecting "turf," position power, and politics are eliminated almost completely. Meresman reiterates, "We don't do that here."

What results is sometimes described as organized chaos. Different teams have different ways of getting there, but the company's vision and direction are well established and clearly understood.

However, there are limits to this discretion, and one is a comprehensive policy for revenue recognition. In the company, there are very few absolutes, but this is one of them. For integrity of the company's financial statements, there can be no compromise, so rules are spelled out explicitly in a widely distributed written policy. There is no individual discretion in gray areas that require the approval of financial executives if revenue is to be recognized. Following this policy is a condition of employment.

Also, empowerment does not mean giving up necessary controls. Division controllers try to enlist the company's auditors to help them with problems, rather than treating them as police.

Information Sharing

Within the company, just about everyone should be able to get financial information about their divisions, and relevant information about others, without having to explain why they need it. It is important for people to remember that divisions are not competing and need to help each other. There is no division name on the company stock they own.

An annual worldwide controller's conference, lasting a week, fosters both information sharing and camaraderie. With people from 30 countries and many different cultures, it is a learning experience for all participants. Ample time is allowed so that people can get to know each other informally.

Leadership Training

The company is constantly thinking about its organizational structure. It wants to ensure that it is organized for the future rather than the past. It continues to focus on hiring the best people and developing successful leaders from its managers. One of the company's more innovative management training and development programs is called SGI 2000. Designed to prepare managers to be leaders within SGI's culture, it is taught by the company's senior executives. In addition, consultants are hired for some leadership exercises and a business simulation game. For each attendee, questionnaires on leadership and management ability are filled out by bosses, peers, subordinates, and others. Each person has a complete assessment and specified development goals and is encouraged to discuss the results in small groups.

Meresman, who serves as a leader and mentor for some of these seminars, finds it helpful once in a while to get out of the normal work environment and think about these things. Doing it as a group helps build working relationships. He describes a particularly effective series of role-play business simulations in which people switched roles and in the process got to know and respect each other. In one, members of a team developed what appeared to be a good business strategy until the finance person told them that they would go broke in a year given their projected cash flow burn rate. This helped them all think about the value of their finance colleagues. People sometimes exhibited different styles while playing different functional roles, and sometimes they forgot to do things that are important in the SGI culture, such as communicating.

Finance Professionals in Teams

Finance professionals are members of many teams at the same time—functional finance teams, division teams, geographic teams, and special-purpose teams focusing on tasks such as the integration of MIPS Technologies, Inc., process improvement, quality, new product introduction, shortening cycle times, data integrity, fixed asset tracking, new information systems, training, employee recognition, career development, and compensation.

Teams have the authority to make things happen. They can assess how a particular issue will cut through the organization and circulate a list of what needs to be done and who needs to do it. "Here's your part, and this is what we need from you." The reason it makes sense and is a priority is the only authority a team really needs.

Partnerships

SGI is at the core of numerous partnerships and strategic alliances, including customers, vendors, software partners, and even employees.

Customers act as partners and technology drivers. Customer needs provide the impetus for product development and enhancements. For example, a film maker may want to do certain special effects that require new capabilities not yet available in SGI's computer systems.

Product development cycle times are short in this business. SGI deliberately shortens the development cycle further to stay ahead of the competition and to incorporate the latest technology. Additionally, SGI's strategy is to cannibalize its own products before a competitor can. SGI will start a crash program to develop the next generation of products 18 months before the planned introduction time. The benefit of shorter cycle time is that more advanced technology is available and the market is clearer than if the project were started 36 months before planned introduction. In this way, the product will be closer to the leading edge of technology and better suited to the target market when it is introduced.

SGI does itself what is strategic to the business—where it adds value or where it is or can be world-class—and subcontracts non-strategic activities to outside vendors. The company has a philosophy that if it can't be world-class at something, then it should partner with an organization that is. It develops relationships with partners who add value and who are world-class in what they do. For example, the company is world-class at designing microprocessors, but does not manufacture its own chips because investing in fabricating equipment is not the best use of its capital, and there are semiconductor companies that are world-class at producing chips. Therefore, SGI has close relationships with six semiconductor manufacturers. Another benefit of the partnership is that when parts are short, SGI can usually get what it needs. However, the company must also understand the position of its partners and ensure that the relationships remain mutually beneficial.

Centralized and Decentralized Finance Function

SGI's finance function is largely decentralized and matrix managed. The company has seven product divisions and 24 international subsidiaries. Up to four finance people are assigned to a product division, and each manufacturing center has about 15 finance people. An average of three to four finance people work in each country subsidiary. Division controllers report straight line to division managers and dotted line to the parent corporate controller.

Most general managers view division controllers as critical members of their teams. In most cases the controllers are considered business partners to their general managers, and that is how they are measured. Although a division controller generally has a "can-do" attitude, he or she can use best judgment and say no to a division general manager, knowing that the corporate controller and CFO will support that decision.

A careful assessment has been made of which activities should be centralized and which decentralized. Activities such as cost accounting for the manufacturing organization and profitability analysis for the divisions are considered to add value to the product and country divisions and are therefore decentralized. Other activities, such as payroll and accounts payable, that do not add value to the divisions or have potential economies of scale are centralized. Rather than encumbering the divisions with their own financing, corporate treasury borrows centrally, makes lease-or-buy decisions, and charges the divisions for asset utilization. Country operations are responsible for achieving local currency financial results against their local currency plans, and international division management is responsible for delivering dollar results. Treasury office is responsible for external hedging contracts on behalf of the corporation.

Recruiting and Hiring

Because of its size and industry reputation, SGI can attract senior financial people with relevant experience in other companies. It tries to hire the best and the brightest. A few are hired directly from business school, but because of the company's fast growth, many of the open slots are for experienced financial professionals and managers.

Functional competence and demonstrated accomplishments are necessary. But in addition, Stan Meresman looks for people who are "all-around athletes" with attributes that fit SGI's culture.

The people who flourish are those who want to make a difference and don't need a lot of management attention. They are people who can understand the company's vision and goals, are comfortable in an unstructured environment, and do not need a lot of direction and supervision. They find out what they need to know, get concurrence when appropriate, use their own initiative to make things happen, and like to be held accountable for the results. They must be comfortable working in a matrix-managed organization. This requires influencing and leadership skills. They must be able to articulate and demonstrate what is best for the company, not just for their division or themselves. They must be comfortable living with ambiguity and constant change.

From 6 to 10 people at SGI talk to each new candidate. This helps SGI evaluate the candidate, but also, over the course of four or five visits to the company, the candidate gets a clear picture of the SGI culture and what it expects from finance professionals. It also allows a candidate to select in or out based on feedback from the interview process. The company doesn't want a new hire to be surprised by the working environment, and it considers itself partly to blame when a new person is not successful.

Ten percent of SGI's labor force is temporary. This helps the company minimize the probability of future layoffs of its regular staff by creating a buffer. (SGI has not had a layoff during the past 10 years, excluding its merger.) It also serves as a good recruiting tool; some outstanding temporary people are hired for regular positions, but only after the normal extensive interviewing process.

Career Paths

There is not much movement between finance and general management of the divisions because most general managers, as well as marketing and sales people, have an electrical engineering background. However, finance personnel in the divisions, in international positions, and in manufacturing are encouraged to explore opportunities within corporate finance and vice versa. A finance person who has corporate, divisional, and field experience is a very valuable member of the organization.

Performance Appraisals and Compensation Reviews

Everyone is evaluated by his or her manager in a written performance review once each year. Generally the manager receives input from peers and a number of other people.

Everyone's salary is reviewed twice a year. Most people receive salary increases annually, but outstanding performers may receive midyear increases. Every full-time employee receives a stock option upon hiring and is eligible to participate in an employee stock purchase plan via payroll deductions. The intent is to have everyone feel like an owner and share in the success of the company.

Meeting objectives and getting results comes first. How you got there comes next. You can always work on polishing the edges. The best performers have an impact on the company beyond their immediate areas of responsibility.

Providing feedback to employees is critical in the evaluation process. The performance appraisal form has a section for development needs and a development action plan. This helps employees understand what steps they need to take to make a greater contribution to the organization and to grow professionally.

When new opportunities arise for people, they may be promoted if they have an 80 percent chance of being successful in their new positions. If their chances of success are only 50 percent, it is probably too early to promote them. Stan Meresman related one case of a prospective manager who was considered to have only a 50 percent chance of succeeding. He and his boss developed a game plan to increase the likelihood of success to 80 percent. The game plan worked, and he was successful in the new position. Meresman adds, "If someone fails, we have failed. We take career development seriously."

President's Club and Spirit of SGI Group

SGI, like many companies, gives special recognition and rewards to its top sales producers. This group, called the President's Club, is treated to a four-day vacation trip, including some working sessions, with top management each year. The trip is meant to be a reward, but there is also an opportunity to talk in an informal environment about how business is going.

What is a little more unusual is a parallel group called the Spirit of SGI Group. Members of this group are nominated by their peers and selected by management. They are considered those who best exemplify the Spirit of SGI—people who are proactive and make things happen. It is not meant to be a popularity contest. This year, there were 45 people in the group, about 1 percent of the employee population.

Members of this group fly in from all parts of the world for a four-day get-together. Each may bring a guest. Last year the group went to a resort in Hawaii. Because of the dollars and executive time committed, the event conveys the message that management really means what it says about the Spirit of SGI. Members of the group can get to know each other and top management on a first-name basis, perhaps sitting next to the president at breakfast or talking to the CFO around the pool. These are opinion leaders who can speak for themselves and also represent their peers' points of view. They are encouraged to speak up, and management is sometimes surprised by what it hears—perhaps things it has been oblivious to.

A major objective of the trip is to talk with the winners about how to maintain the SGI culture. In a workshop, questions are asked such as, "What are some of the things we don't want to lose as the company gets bigger? What makes the company special? What are you most proud of? Why do you want to work here? What gives you job satisfaction? What do we need to fix? What undesirable things are starting to creep in?" From the workshop discussion a list of action items is developed for management to implement and report back to the group.

The Spirit of SGI Group allows a number of effective and concerned people in various parts and at different levels of the organization an opportunity they would not otherwise have to get to know each other and members of top management. By encouraging such a network of acquaintances to develop and by maintaining an open-door policy, top management has given people throughout the organization the ability to speak up when they have suggestions or see something that does not seem right. Management believes that this is an important way to maintain the entrepreneurial spirit and open communication that underlie the company's culture.

12

Steelcase Inc.

Interview Subjects: *Alwyn Rougier-Chapman, senior vice president–finance; Robert E. Hubling, vice president–treasurer; William Williams, vice president–controller*

Executive Summary

Steelcase decided to make some changes while it was financially strong. It recognized that the office furnishing business was becoming more competitive and broadened the definition of its business to helping people work more effectively wherever they work. Steelcase is focusing its product development on the needs of the knowledge worker and applying the insight it gains to the way its own employees work together. Former CEO Frank Merlotti spearheaded a world-class manufacturing program in 1987. Under the current CEO, Jerry Myers, a broader world-class performance program now includes functions such as finance.

Steelcase has made a strong commitment to teamwork. There are some 800 self-managed teams in the company. Virtually everyone in the company is a member of a team. Team participation is usually in addition to a person's normal duties. The finance function has participated with other functions such as marketing, sales, manufacturing, distribution, and information systems in reengineering and continuous improvement teams. Those teams have examined processes such as purchasing, invoicing, accounts payable, returns and allowances, concession quote pricing, and closing the books at the end of the month.

Through experience, Steelcase has developed useful guidelines on how to organize and direct teams. Teams are encouraged to stay customer focused, to direct their efforts toward problems they can realistically solve, to avoid spending time on issues over which they have no control, and to disband when their missions have been accomplished.

Background

Founded in 1912, Steelcase is the largest office furniture manufacturer in the United States, with a 21 percent market share. The company is private, virtually debt-free, and finances its growth internally. For the fiscal year that ended in February 1993, sales were $1.8 billion consolidated and $2.5 billion worldwide, including joint ventures. The company employs 8,000 people in the Grand Rapids area, 13,000 in North America, and 17,000 worldwide, including joint ventures. Steelcase North America has recently become the largest company in the United States and Canada to achieve International Standards Organization (ISO) 9001 registration under a single certificate. This certification, in the words of Steelcase North America President Rob Pew, "signifies Steelcase products are manufactured under a consistent internationally recognized quality system."

Changing While Ahead

Steelcase has undergone a cultural change process in the past several years, spanning the tenure of two CEOs. It began about 1987 when then CEO Frank Merlotti saw that the industry was becoming more competitive and that Steelcase would have to make some changes to protect its leadership position. Merlotti warned of the danger of complacency, particularly for a company such as Steelcase that is a leader in its industry and that, as a private company, is shielded from the scrutiny of Wall Street analysts. He said that it is too easy for top executives of large organizations to avoid making changes. To find out where change is needed, they need to listen to people in the factory and people who deal with customers. He said that it is easier for a company to make changes when it is healthy, as Steelcase fortunately is, and that change should not be a program, but a way of life.

CEO's Management Principles

In 1987, Merlotti articulated five management principles that were the foundation for a world-class manufacturing program:

- Quality
- Faster throughput
- Elimination of waste
- Product group focus
- Employee involvement

Self-Managed Teams in the Factory

The fifth principle, employee involvement, was the basis for the company's initiative to create a team-based organization in the factory. Factories became product focused. Work cells in the factories assumed responsibility for products. The company learned about teams through experience; some teams were successful and others were not. Some teams found that they did not have the ability to control the problems they were meant to solve. Others found that the problems they were looking at were not really the core problems that needed to be addressed. Now, virtually everyone working in a Steelcase factory is part of a team.

New CEO's Principles and Values

Jerry K. Myers, a former TRW executive, became CEO of Steelcase at the end of 1990. His principles, values, and strategic objectives were consistent with Merlotti's and were clearly articulated in a number of documents prepared for employees, shareholders, and other stakeholders.

Myers believes that a company's vision should be based on its core beliefs and values. The values he has defined include the following:

- □ Satisfying customers completely
- □ Treating ourselves and each other with respect
- □ Valuing and building the diversity of our workforce
- □ Working as partners with customers, fellow employees, design professionals, dealers, suppliers, and shareholders
- □ Supporting our communities
- □ Respecting the environment
- □ Acting with integrity in everything we do

Myers has defined a number of strategic objectives for Steelcase:

- □ Performing at world-class levels in all aspects of our business
- □ Having an organization that is flexible and fast on its feet
- □ Empowering employees to make decisions on their own and take responsibility for quality and service to their clients
- □ Achieving market coverage, speed, and accuracy

Consistent with those objectives, he has defined seven specific goals:

- □ Reduce reasons for customer complaints to four per million opportunities
- □ Reduce product development time to 10 months
- □ Achieve two-week customer cycle time
- □ Reduce costs by 30 percent
- □ Reduce safety incidents by 90 percent
- □ Reduce waste by eliminating 75 percent of what we throw away today
- □ Reduce quality audits by 80 percent

Myers observes that we have entered a knowledge economy. People will have access to a constantly broadening range of information. Products will be more easily customized and people will demand more simplicity in the way they are accessed and delivered. There will be a scarcity of and increasing competition for knowledge workers. The boundaries between business, home, and social lives will continue to blur, and the work culture will have to support personal and family values.

Myers sees the corporate community that Steelcase serves moving away from hierarchical and authoritarian organizations. Office environments must now accommodate teams as well as individuals. Knowledge workers are defining product requirements. They will control work environments and reconfigure them at will. They will want to use their office tools in airplanes, cars, and homes.

Steelcase's strategy to compete in this changing environment is to broaden the definition of its business to helping people work more effectively wherever they work. It is focusing on the physical, social, and informational elements of the knowledge worker's environment, observing, measuring, and managing the entire system for knowledge productivity. With the continuing objective of exhibiting flexibility and speed in responding to customer needs, it is organizing around processes rather than functions.

World-class manufacturing has been redefined as world-class performance, and it includes reengineering and continuous improvement activities throughout the company, including the finance function. In this redefinition, the company took the conscious step of telling its employees that quality is not a manufacturing issue but a corporate issue. If the product is right but the billing is wrong, the customer won't be happy.

Finance Function Mission and Vision

Alwyn Rougier-Chapman says that the finance function mission has not changed very much recently, but the vision has. It is recognized that people have gone through tough times in the recent recession and the company's first-ever downsizing. They need to reach their potential and also have fun. The finance function Vision and Mission Statement in figure 20 is meant to be a challenge that's impossible to reach. If the company reaches the challenge, it will have to change the vision.

FIGURE 20: Finance Function Mission and Vision

Mission

To provide the highest quality, proactive, innovative, cost-effective, timely, value-added service to the corporation, including all of its stakeholders and the Steelcase family of businesses, by being a full business partner.

The activities which contribute to the well-being of the corporation will include but are not limited to:

Policies and procedures
Planning
Business advice and counsel
Establishing and maintaining systems of internal control
Processing, recording, and reporting
Compliance
Evaluation and analysis
Safeguarding of assets
Enhancing the value of assets
Investment and resource allocation
Establishing measure criteria
Maintaining liquidity
Enhancing shareholder value

Vision

To be so superior at serving our customers that we are recognized by all as a world-class benchmark for the quality and effectiveness of the function.

To be the service organization of choice in the corporation with a diverse, educated, motivated staff providing leading-edge concepts, processes, techniques, and solutions. To be recognized and respected as being business people responsive to the management needs of the corporation. To be recognized by every employee in the corporation as the function to be part of or in teamwork with, since we will be known as the function which is intellectually stimulating, given responsibility, where all may reach their potential and all have fun doing so.

Finance People in Business Unit Organization

The finance function has always had both a corporate and a divisional role. Until recently, the company had cross-functional groups called business management groups that were concerned with new products and changes in product lines. There was always a finance person, a development person, a manufacturing person, and a marketing person in those groups. Their primary focus was new products and changes in product lines.

Steelcase's business in North America was recently divided into five business units—four product units and one geographic unit. These five units market and sell their products through a common marketing and sales organization, but otherwise have complete responsibility for their businesses. The new structure created a need for greater teamwork. The finance function has put people out in the field, in the plants, and in domestic and overseas sales subsidiaries. Each business unit manager has direct reports from about 10 functions including the business unit controller. Finance people are involved in cross-functional teams addressing issues such as cost reduction, new products, and marketing programs. The duties and responsibilities of business unit finance groups are described in figure 21.

FIGURE 21: **Business Unit Finance Group Duties and Responsibilities**

Support Product Development Process

- ☐ Engineering Support Request/Manufacturing Support Request (ESR/MSRs), product pricing, target profitability goals, Design for Competitiveness (DFC)
- ☐ Return on investment, discounted cash flow, economic justifications, and other analyses

Improved Product Costing

- ☐ Departmental burdens
- ☐ Activity-based costing (ABC)
- ☐ Total manufacturing cost model (TMCM)
- ☐ Focus factory accounting
- ☐ Labor by product

Budgeting

- ☐ Income statement and limited balance sheet for business unit
- ☐ Departmental budgeting
- ☐ Manufacturing budgeting
- ☐ Product-line budgeting (future)
- ☐ Materials (commodity) budgeting

Cost Accounting

- ☐ Monthly cost of sales
- ☐ Inventory valuation and management
- ☐ Cost builds
- ☐ Database management and integrity
- ☐ Pricing

FIGURE 21: **Business Unit Finance Group Duties and Responsibilities (continued)**

- ☐ System maintenance
- ☐ Plant accounting
- ☐ Variance analysis—material and labor
- ☐ Labor distribution
- ☐ Year-end inventory

Financial Reporting/Managerial Accounting

- ☐ Income statement and balance sheet
- ☐ Gross operating profits by plant
- ☐ Inventory analysis
- ☐ Factory labor efficiency
- ☐ Profitability by product series (plant, series, business unit)
- ☐ Departmental expenses
- ☐ Scrap reporting
- ☐ Manufacturing statistics
- ☐ Materials price increases and decreases

Management Authorization Request (MAR) Processing

- ☐ Approvals and procedures

Empowerment, Teamwork, and Quality

Bill Williams, controller, believes that Steelcase is still young in defining what empowerment is, living it, and getting people to understand and embrace it. If you asked 15 managers what it is, you would probably get 15 different answers. The senior management of the company has recognized that it cannot husband all the responsibility for making decisions. Responsibility and decision making are being pushed closer to the customer. But this is a culture shock to an organization in which decisions have been made at the top. The reward systems necessary to nurture and facilitate empowerment are not yet in place throughout the organization. Management is still grappling with what it means; then it has to be disseminated to all levels. Within finance, the reengineering teams, continuous improvement teams, and self-directed work teams are a start. When management sponsors a team, it is saying, "Here is an area where we are going to empower you. We are going to give you time and resources to work in this area. We want to see some improvement. You are going to come back and tell us what your goal is, how you are going to organize your work, what you need from us to help you do that."

Alwyn Rougier-Chapman believes that the values behind empowerment and teamwork will ultimately transcend total quality and world-class performance, but that has not yet been recognized at Steelcase. He sees four layers:

- Direction
- Empowerment
- Teamwork
- Process

It is difficult for one layer to be effective if the others are not in place. There is no point in teamwork or quality goals without a process to work on. But the team does not have the latitude to do its work without empowerment, and an empowered team's effort will not be properly focused without direction.

Control and Empowerment

In the view of Bill Williams, "With empowerment, we have identified who owns and has responsibility for a process. They take responsibility for the improvement of that process. That does not mean I as a manager in the function am not interested in what they do, or that there is not the accountability for results." There must be audits, controls, separation of duties—even with self-managed teams. Williams believes the concepts are compatible. Taking responsibility for improving a process is not in conflict with letters of authority, sign-offs, internal controls, and proper business practices. What has changed is that neither control nor quality are viewed today as one-off responsibilities. Quality and controls are being built into day-to-day jobs.

Empowerment and teamwork can actually increase controls because more people are aware of the controls that are necessary. Williams also believes that getting people involved in defining the boundaries of a process such as order fulfillment and who owns it facilitates control. It causes people to operate more within the scope of their defined responsibility. Management is not abdicating its leadership role, nor is it being overly restrictive. People are given freedom within their circles of responsibility to do their work and not look to others above to make all their decisions for them.

Sharing Financial Information

As a private company, Steelcase has historically not disclosed financial information to the public. Internally, information has been shared mostly on a need-to-know basis. A Dun & Bradstreet report is filed. The company gives the community an indication of how the business is doing—for example, citing the number of people employed—but does not disclose profits. Some earnings information was leaked in the course of a shareholder meeting last year; this was the first time the press had ever seen any financial information about the company.

Now, management realizes that it cannot empower its employees and maintain good customer alliances without making more information available. Bill Williams describes an explosion of information compared with three years ago. Steelcase North America President Rob Pew now holds meetings for the supervisory staff in a local high school auditorium to review the profit and loss (P&L) numbers. He represents the third generation of his family involved in Steelcase management. His viewpoint is different from that of his father, who thought that the financials of a private company were the business of the owners and top management only. Rob Pew was influenced by president and CEO Jerry Myers, who came from a public company and was accustomed to sharing financial information with employees.

Increasing Financial Literacy

One goal of the Controller's Group is to increase the financial literacy of the company, from senior management to the front-level associates. Financial information is shared to help managers of other functions such as the business units do their jobs more effectively. One example is a report prepared by the internal finance company on the number of projects financed and the number of dealers involved; it is shared internally and externally. Another example is an estimate of profitability by program type (e.g., 48-hour or 12-day), by selling organization (e.g., Education and Institutional, Export, Government, Principal Accounts), by business unit (e.g., Wood, Systems, Case Goods), by product line (e.g., System 9000, Sensor Chair), and by worldwide alliance (very large organizations that Steelcase serves on a worldwide basis). Outside the finance function, the Dealer Alliance Group provides a comparative operations review that contains financial ratios that dealers can use for benchmarking. The report is broken down by type of dealer, such as furniture or general line.

Performance Measures: What Is Driving the Results

The finance function has been asked to take a leadership role in defining performance measurements to be used throughout the company. Finance is defining measures that go beyond the traditional P&L to tell units how they are doing as businesses—not just what results are, but what is driving the results. Principles behind the new performance measures the finance function is designing are explained in figure 22. The finance function has recommended a new group of performance measures, which are described in figure 23.

FIGURE 22: Performance Measures: Guiding Principles

Provide a balanced scorecard of how the business is doing, falling into four "buckets:"

- ☐ Financial
- ☐ Customer
- ☐ Internal
- ☐ Innovation

An example of a measure in the innovation bucket is a breakdown of how much of current product volume was developed within the last year, two years, and five years.

- ☐ Shift from a preponderance of results-oriented measures to a balance of results and process measures.
- ☐ Use fewer rather than more measures.
- ☐ Delta and trend is more important than absolute.
- ☐ Cascade through organization, incorporating into process identification and ownership efforts.
- ☐ Measurement system should capture and convey
  - Trend
  - Where we are today
  - Goals, short-term and long-term

FIGURE 22: Performance Measures: Guiding Principles (continued)

- ☐ Four types of measures are needed:
  - Quality
  - Cost or financial
  - Yield or productivity (inputs/outputs)
  - Time
- ☐ Every process should have a handful of measures, using at least three of these types.
- ☐ Measures must be timely.

Based on these guiding principles, the finance function has recommended a new group of performance measures. They are described in figure 23.

FIGURE 23: Recommended Quantitative Measures

Description of Measure	*Type of Measure*
Sales, gross and net (by business unit, product, and selling organization)	Growth
Operating income	Profitability
Return on net assets/Return on controllable assets	Profitability
Operating cash flow	Liquidity
Market share, by segment	Overall barometer of competitiveness, customer satisfaction, and value
Daily report card (quality and delivery)	Customer, process oriented
Order-to-delivery cycle time	Quality, process capability
Sales per employee	Productivity; measurable against peer companies
Defects per million (manufacturing)	Quality, process oriented
Hours per unit	Manufacturing productivity
Product cost and operating expense as a percentage of sales	Cost and expense management
Working capital and fixed capital turns	Asset productivity, operating efficiency, and asset utilization
New product (developed within the past one, two, or five years) sales as percentage of total sales	Innovation

The measures in figure 23 are designed to help Steelcase management answer on a continuous basis a number of vital questions related to business performance and where improvements are needed, such as the following:

- How are we doing versus competition?
- Are we growing and where?
- Are we profitable and why?
- Are we effectively managing assets?
- Are we controlling operating expenses?
- What is our product quality and conversion process capability?
- What is our order fulfillment process quality?
- How are new products contributing?
- Are we increasing or destroying shareholder value?
- Is value added by our people going up or down?

The challenges ahead are to make sure that information and not just data is produced, to make sure the information is timely and accessible to people who need it, and to train people to understand and use the information.

Bill Williams believes that the very process of sharing information on all of the projects the finance function is working on—virtually all of them cross-functional—is helping to break down silos.

Hiring and Measuring Finance Professionals

In hiring for his group, Williams looks for people who are smart and energetic, have good communication and problem-solving skills, and have a generalist orientation to business. Interpersonal skills and adaptability to the team environment are implicit hiring criteria, though not spelled out. These criteria are considered on a par with knowledge, technical skills, and just being a hard worker. Many managers have spent their entire working lives at Steelcase. Williams believes the company can benefit from people from the outside who know nothing about furniture but can bring new perspectives on management as well as a strong knowledge base.

Several people are involved in interviewing each candidate, and several people are consulted in the performance evaluation process. For example, Williams may check on how well a financial analyst is supporting internal customers in distribution and marketing. Williams wants to see people get outside their narrowly defined jobs, look at businesses in a strategic way, and be customer focused.

Finance Teams in Business Units

The business unit organization created greater need for teamwork. There are now approximately 800 self-managed teams throughout the company. Because of the business unit structure, the finance function owns very few processes. When teams set out to improve processes, they work with members of the business units and try to develop procedures that can be adapted to all of the business units. Finance people are involved in teams looking at a variety of issues such as cost reduction, new products, and new marketing programs.

Corporate Development Center: Top-Level Capital Budgeting Decision

Nowhere could teams be more effective than in product development. In the past, designers, engineers, marketers, and others involved in product development worked in different locations as parts of different functions in the organization. Product development time and the whole creative process could be improved if all of these people could be brought together. This was the inspiration behind the Corporate Development Center, which was opened in 1989. It was designed from the inside out. Members of cross-functional product design teams are located close together in "neighborhoods." Open spaces and common areas allow them to work together. The center allows the company to model the knowledge worker's total office environment in line with CEO Myers' core strategy to "practice what we do and sell."

The decision to build the center is an example of teamwork at the highest level. It was beyond the boundaries of the usual capital budgeting process. Normally, project requests start, bottom up, from plants and departments. They must be properly supported with both a quantitative analysis and business justification. Approval is top down. There is a prioritization process, which is influenced by the total amount of the capital budget. In the case of the Corporate Development Center, the original cost was estimated in accordance with the defined process. Successively higher estimates were sent to the board and approved. The investment decision went to the basic roots of the direction the company was going. They were driven by a philosophy and a need, not by how much the company wanted to spend.

Reengineering Teams

The company began to establish reengineering teams, both within functions and across functions, four years ago. A reengineering group is made up of a core group that has been pulled out of line responsibility completely. It is supported by line people who are members of subteams.

The team maps out entire processes, starting with the customer, going through every functional step, and looping back to the customer. It visits other companies for benchmarking. (Motorola and Harley-Davidson are two companies recently visited by Steelcase teams.) It looks for redundancies and non-value-added activities. It redesigns work processes using current technology. The finance person brings functional knowledge to the team and is also involved with all business issues.

Purchasing, Receiving, and Accounts Payable System (PRAPS)

PRAPS is an example what reengineering teams have created in the finance function. A team including production inventory control (part of manufacturing), purchasing, distribution, accounts payable, and information services people reengineered the entire buying, receiving, invoicing, and paying process. It also examined the vendor performance and evaluation process. Factory and purchasing people spent time in accounts payable, and accounts payable people spent time in receiving. The greatest impact of the team effort has been on efficiency and quality. For example, faster processing of bills improves the efficiency of the buying process. The new process provides a platform for EDI, which reduces cycle time. PRAPS has created some additional work because controls have been tightened.

At the outset, PRAPS was endorsed by the CEO both verbally and in writing. It was cosponsored by the CFO, on behalf of the finance function, and by the purchasing function. The team reported to a management committee made up of the functional groups for the purposes of oversight and communication. The committee met with the entire team to avoid "interpretive" communication and to deal with the issues in front of all those involved. Later, an implementation/design team was assigned; it included employees at all levels of the functions involved in the process. Then, user teams consisting of both volunteers and assigned personnel were formed for ongoing implementation.

Team members became exposed to concerns outside their narrow job functions, learned as they went, and gained an understanding of the problems. Different personalities worked through conflict and resistance. Overall, results of the team effort were considered positive, except perhaps for the amount of time the project required. Management recognized that all teams need to be disbanded after some point in time, because otherwise their creativity diminishes. New teams are required to encourage open thinking and new ideas. The experience of this team was useful input for the team training process.

Customer Fulfillment Order Entry Process

Another example of reengineering teams involving the finance function is the redesign of the customer fulfillment order entry process. Billing adjustment people from treasury have been particularly useful team members because their job exposes them to every part of the process from the time the customer enters an order until the product is shipped and the customer pays.

Teams within finance are reengineering the financial planning, budgeting, and forecasting process; the closing, consolidation, and financial reporting process; and the capital appropriation process.

Continuous Improvement Teams

Continuous improvement teams are an ongoing activity in all parts of the company including the finance function. Cross-functional teams with members from the Controller's Group and business units have addressed closing the books, accounts payable, and payroll. They identify customers, which are mostly internal, try to understand customer requirements, map every process, define outputs, and develop measures for how well the customers are being satisfied.

Continuous improvement teams work on two levels. Project teams of experienced senior managerial and professional people are hand picked to reengineer processes. They disband when they have accomplished their stated objective. Permanent teams run the reengineered processes.

Several examples illustrate how continuous improvement teams have examined and improved processes:

Closing the Books at the End of the Month

A team selected and implemented new accounting software for consolidation after comparing different vendors' products. The result was a reduction in monthly closing time from 13 days to 10. The company expects that enhancements will reduce the closing time further.

Returns and Allowances Report

The original report did not provide enough information on the causes for returns and allowances. The "reason" code in the report did not allow enough options, nor was it sufficiently descriptive. Finance was the owner and sponsor of the project. Team members from finance, information services, and manufacturing discussed the needs of people responsible for manufacturing and quality. Information services changed the software and the format of the report so that users would have more flexibility in filling it out, information would be more accessible, and the information would help in avoiding future problems through corrective action. Users had thought that the root of the problems was in manufacturing, but when the reason codes were further broken down, it turned out that most of the adjustments were generated in the sales and order entry areas. This finding illustrated that not all quality problems are in the plant and that numerous people and functions are involved in meeting customer needs.

Concession Quote Pricing

Team members were frontline operations people at all levels from sales, sales services, and manufacturing (quality). The owner and sponsor of the project was originally the Quality Council, and toward the end, Sales. The project scope was to define problems and opportunities with pricing procedures and documentation. The result of the team effort was reduced pricing errors on customer acknowledgments and invoices. There is now more emphasis on the work done up front when the order is received, on better quality, and on productivity. The team worked well together, but the biggest problem was persuading managers from different functions to commit the time required of people reporting to them. Finding the resources to keep the team going was a constant selling job. The lesson learned was that an executive sponsor is needed right from the beginning. The sales executive who later sponsored the project had more clout than the Quality Council had in the beginning.

Other continuous improvement teams are forming and have begun implementing self-directed work teams in accounts payable and payroll accounting. They are also reducing the closing process cycle time by accelerating the interface of sales, accounting, and accounts receivable with the general ledger.

How Teams Are Created and Managed

Suggestions for creating teams come from all levels, from business unit and function heads and from other managers and staff members. There can be any number of reasons to create a team—an idea for a new product, a marketing program, or a way to reduce costs. Management may decide to form a team and select the members, or a self-managed team may be formed by volunteers. Members may all come from a business unit, such as the chair unit, or they may be drawn from a number of other functions such as finance.

Membership on a team is always in addition to regular job responsibilities and work requirements. Practically every person in the top half of the organization is assigned to a team. It would be possible to place every person in a traditional organizational chart and then overlay a chart showing all the teams they belonged to—almost a dual organization structure.

When teams were first organized in the factory, supervisors were appointed as team leaders. Now many teams throughout the company elect their own leaders or share leadership among their members. The company tries to train all team members so that the teams will be self-directed. For example, a team that has reorganized accounts payable does not have a supervisor, but encourages each member to take responsibility for the activities related to his or her total assignment.

Alwyn Rougier-Chapman observes that teams will not work if they are not directed properly. A manager convening a team must make expectations clear. Self-convening teams must make their missions clear. Teams in the finance function are expected to define their parameters and expectations at the outset and to have a specific focus, such as a process with the objective of achieving a measurable improvement in results. Teams are asked not to waste time on things like corporate policies that are on the perimeter of the problems they are working on. Also, as management learned with the PRAPS project, teams are expected to achieve their objectives within defined time frames or disband. Management tries to deter teams from a tendency toward self-perpetuation.

FIGURE 24: **Finance Action Team Guidelines**

Definition

An action team is a group of employees performing similar work who volunteer to meet regularly to learn about and apply basic improvement tools and techniques. They use these techniques to identify problems within their control, analyze them, and recommend solutions to management. When possible, they will initiate the action necessary to implement the solution. Normally, teams consist of from three to six employees from the same work area.

Purpose and Outcome

- ☐ More effective teamwork
- ☐ Employee participation and job involvement
- ☐ Personal and professional skill development
- ☐ Reduce errors and enhance quality
- ☐ Reduce costs
- ☐ Increase productivity and departmental effectiveness

FIGURE 24: Finance Action Team Guidelines (continued)

Responsibilities

A steering committee is normally established to set objectives for the action team program, develop and oversee the program, control the rate of expansion, arrange for training, and monitor the overall effectiveness of the program. The team consists of the senior vice president, his staff, and managers from the controller and treasury functions. The team meets once per quarter, or more often if needed. The manager's term is one year.

A trained facilitator from human resources is responsible for coordinating and directing action team activities and training team leaders. (Eventually, there will be facilitators within the finance function.)

Team leaders provide leadership for the teams, teach techniques to team members, maintain appropriate records, and assume overall responsibility for the operation of their teams. The initial team leader is normally the supervisor of the area concerned. The leader ensures proper communication with management through such means as meeting minutes, activity reports, and management presentations by teams.

Managers who have teams in their areas are responsible for responding quickly to team requests and recommendations. When it is not possible for them to comply, they provide an explanation. Approved team recommendations are implemented with a minimum of delay. Managers have the right and responsibility to verify the cost effectiveness of team recommendations. Whenever possible, team activities should be aligned with organizational goals.

Team members direct their attention to problems and projects under their control, ensure participation of all team members, use action team techniques, and consider workload when scheduling team meetings.

Teams have the right to recommend prioritization of problems or projects regardless of the source. They attempt to identify, analyze, and implement solutions to problems. If management approval is necessary, they do not proceed until it has been obtained. Team members attempt to improve communication, collaboration, and involvement among all members as well as among other employees. They conduct presentations to their management and then to the steering committee regarding specific recommendations, accomplishments, or the status of the team's work.

Policy

Team members do not address subjects that are not within their area of control, such as personalities, wages, benefits and discipline, employment, and termination policies.

Teams meet at least one hour a week, preferably during normal working hours. If it is not possible to meet during normal working hours, overtime is paid according to standard policy.

Employees volunteer to become team members. Nonmembers are free to suggest problems to teams as possibilities for analysis.

Team members are allowed to attend other team meetings when invited to work on joint problems.

Facilities, equipment, and supplies are provided to teams to ensure effective meetings.

Team meetings have high priority, and team members are encouraged to attend them. The autonomy of teams is respected by following the "hands off/fair game" rule. Once a team has begun to identify the problems to work on, hands off until it has a chance to either solve it or select another problem. Once a team has selected its problem, items on its original list become fair game.

FIGURE 25: Action Team Steps

Set meeting date(s) and time(s).

Team leader takes team through the five modules of the Team Effectiveness Model training course: Mission, Goals, Roles, Procedures, and Relationships.

Team identifies improvement opportunities through brainstorming, interviews, intuition, and analysis of past performance. Current problems, problem disconnects, problem causes and analyses, and possible designs for improved processes are considered.

Team writes problem statements based on the analysis. All team members vote on the relative merit of the projects considered.

Team chooses a project with input from department manager.

Solutions and suggested improvements are selected.

Trial is implemented.

Project results are reported to the manager and success is celebrated.

Manager reports results to his or her supervisor for review by the steering committee.

The process is repeated. All concerned are reminded that world-class performance (WCP) means customer focus and continuous improvement.

FIGURE 26: Guidelines for Improving Team Performance

Information gathering and analysis helps a team identify the most significant improvement opportunities. Problems are selected based on the following criteria:

- ☐ The impact the problem has on the team's customer. Efforts are focused on a problem that significantly affects customer satisfaction.
- ☐ The level of control the team has over the problem and all its components. At this point, activity should center on problems within the

FIGURE 26: Guidelines for Improving Team Performance (continued)

boundaries of the team's control. Cross-functional problem solving occurs later in the WCP effort.

- ☐ The likelihood of success in solving the problem. The team does not begin with a problem that is too complex or difficult. Its goal is to develop confidence in its ability to solve problems and continuously improve.

The team leader helps the team develop a clear statement defining the problem to be attacked and identify the goal the team wants to reach by attacking the problem. Whenever possible, the team quantifies the goal. For example, "Develop a system to respond to all customer messages within one hour."

The team's efforts to gather and analyze information pay off handsomely as the team begins its activity. Teams follow specific steps:

1. Determine the "root" or primary cause of the problem. Avoid the tendency to jump right to solutions without first defining problem causes. The root problem causes are the items or events that cause the majority of the problems. The "80/20" rule often applies here. Teams usually find that a problem is caused 80 percent or more of the time by 20 percent or less of all likely problem causes.

   Team leaders may begin by starting the team to brainstorm a list of likely problem causes. For example, if the team finds it is providing a service or product to its customer eight hours after the request instead of the required four hours, it may brainstorm a list of possible causes. It may gather information on how frequently each cause occurs. It may list all likely problem causes and the frequency of each one on a chart.
2. Develop a solution. Brainstorm potential solutions to the root problem cause, then focus in on a single most likely solution to the problem. Review your solution with all stakeholders—people who are affected by the solution. Review the team's solution with customers to ensure that the team is addressing their real concerns.
3. Test your solution. Provide time to give the solution a trial run, gather performance data on the trial run, and then work out any bugs prior to formal implementation.
4. Plan implementation. Include all the necessary players and actions required to ensure success. Think through alternative approaches should the team run into trouble.
5. Establish performance measures for the new solution. These performance measures are based on customer requirements. Put in place a system to ensure that performance is continuously monitored against the stated goal or measure. Use this measurement to set new goals and help the team continually increase performance over time.

As the team proceeds through these steps, the leader plans positive reinforcement or recognition activities for team members who develop solutions that result in improved performance. Similar activities are planned for the people who are involved in implementing and maintaining solutions over time.

Role of Managers

Managers who are not team members should play no role other than providing advice if asked, or perhaps acting as sponsors. Sponsors oversee teams and make sure they meet their goals, but they do not supervise from day to day. For example, Rougier-Chapman is a co-sponsor of the PRAPS team. The other cosponsor is from purchasing.

When a manager or sponsor does not support a team's recommendation, he or she must give a reason why. If a team has several sponsors and they disagree, they will go to a more senior person such as Rougier-Chapman.

Teamwork Training

Everyone in the finance function has had training in world-class performance, leadership, empowerment, and working in teams. Formal training sessions, led by a facilitator from human resources, cover what it is to be a team, how to define team rules and processes, how to define customers and their needs, how to map processes, and other tools and techniques. Concurrent and related training includes valuing differences and appreciating diversity. The training is supplemented by videos shown at lunchtime. Attendance, though voluntary, has been good. A video on the Harley-Davidson turnaround story was followed by a group discussion. FMN Videos from the Financial Executives Institute have been well received.

Evaluation of Team Organization

The factory is still way ahead of the office at Steelcase in forming and working with teams. In the white-collar area, some people are still reluctant to change and some supervisors still feel threatened.

Most teams formed so far have been composed of managers, supervisors, and strong professional people. The job performance of some people has improved noticeably as a result of their participation on reengineering teams. They have grown, matured, and gained new knowledge and self-confidence. Teams have taken on increased responsibilities without adding staff. Internal performance measures have improved, indicating that the teams must be doing something right. But only about 10 percent of the people in the finance function have been members of teams so far. The team approach has been hampered by an ever-changing population. An employee who has been in a job for six months may post for another job. When people move to new jobs, teams are dissipated, and new teams must be trained in their place.

As the team approach sweeps through the company, Rougier-Chapman wants to make sure that the individual is not lost. It would be unfortunate for the company and its employees to sacrifice individual accountability, initiative, leadership, creativity, and competitiveness.

Organizational Learning

Participation in cross-functional teams has broadened the knowledge of each team member. People who have worked on teams say they know more about the company, more about the industry, and more about what other people and other functions do. They understand why other team members are necessary, whether they are finance people or manufacturing people. It is still too early to evaluate people's improved knowledge as a result of backing each other up and knowing several jobs on a team.

Steelcase believes that individuals in teams have compensating strengths and weaknesses. Each brings unique skills and experiences. To achieve their goals, teams must benefit from this synergy. Team members learn from each other, and learn that they will not get as far acting as "lone rangers."

External Partnerships

Long-term relationships are nothing new at Steelcase. Treasurer Bob Hubling describes a relationship of shared values and objectives with Steelcase's two primary insurance brokers, who act as an extension of the company's own insurance department. Recently, the brokers have switched their pricing from commissions to annual fees, helping Steelcase avoid ups and downs in premium expense and helping underwriters and brokers evaluate their profitability over a several-year period. Hubling believes that the measure of a good relationship is for both parties to feel it is profitable. This philosophy extends to banking relationships, investment dealers, and all vendors through the supply chain.

CEO Jerry Myers recently defined responsibilities for both Steelcase and its dealers for achieving dealer world-class performance:

- Dealers are required to implement their own continuous improvement process, and are helped in doing so by an organization called the Steelcase Quality Alliance.
- Dealer performance is measured by customers and monitored.
- Dealerships are linked electronically to important customers and to Steelcase.
- Dealerships have unquestioned capability in core services and offer additional services such as inventory management, move management, warehousing, renewal, refurbishment, design support, and in some cases, facilities management.
- Dealers handle products such as full-height partitions and are integrated with building systems.
- Dealer personnel are experts on office environment matters.
- Dealers are tightly linked with Steelcase in planning and setting goals.
- Dealers serve customers from stock with same- or next-day delivery and deliver other orders, including those considered custom, within 14 days.

Steelcase has 57 customers called "worldwide alliances" for which it installs and improves office installations throughout the world. Shell and AT&T are examples. In line with its strategy to be the office environment company, Steelcase not only sells furniture but provides other ancillary services as well. For instance, the company has worked with Arthur Andersen Consulting to install information systems and with Peerless Lighting in San Francisco to ensure that their ambient and glare-free lighting systems are designed to complement Steelcase furniture. Finance people work as needed as part of alliance teams. They describe to customers the research the company is doing and explain on an index basis how expenses such as research and development have increased, justifying price increases. They also analyze profitability by worldwide alliance customer.

Steelcase has historically been more vertically integrated than some of its competitors such as Herman Miller. Now the company believes that it cannot afford to keep building new plants as it has in the past. It will have to deal more with partnerships and do more outsourcing. But Rougier-Chapman explains that simply outsourcing what has been done on the inside gets the company nowhere. Logic tells you that it is cheaper to do most things internally than externally. You may believe that you are shifting costs, but you are really shifting profits. The challenge is to keep doing on the inside what the company does best and to outsource where a partner can add value. For example, Steelcase may build housing for lights and install fixtures, but beyond that it does better working in partnership with a company whose expertise is in lighting technology. Part of staying lean is defining your parameters—what you do well, where you can achieve competitive advantage—and doing other things with sensible alliances.

Internal Partnerships

Steelcase has long been regarded as a stable employer with low turnover. Its human resource function recently won an Optimas Award for a workers' compensation strategy that includes on-site physician care and redirection of workers, usually at full pay, to duties they may be more able to perform than their regular jobs during recovery periods. The award is sponsored annually by Tiffany & Company and published in *Personnel Journal.*

When an employee is not performing for any reason, such as drug use, the company does everything possible to bring the person back to being useful in the company and the community. Counseling services are available. When employees become redundant, the company looks for retraining opportunities. This is easier in the blue-collar than in the white-collar area, where training tends to be functional. Within finance, there is some flexibility in moving people among the head office functional staff, the business units, and dealer alliances.

These policies are not always easy to maintain in a period of recession, downsizing, and "rightsizing." Steelcase has had to implement two voluntary layoff programs in the past three years in as humanitarian a way as possible.

To help employees balance their professional and personal lives, the company is receptive within limits to job sharing, flextime, and work at home, depending on the needs of the job. Jobs with budgetary authority or supervisory responsibility typically are not split. However, a few managerial jobs in the company are now held by two people as an experiment to test whether this approach is workable. The job of the CFO's secretary is split between two people. This works well for Alwyn Rougier-Chapman because both people know the job, and when one must be out, there is virtually always a backup. Flextime is popular, particularly in the Michigan summers, which are considered too short. It must be approved within the department to ensure adequate coverage during normal working hours. While the finance function is not philosophically against work at home, it is difficult to implement for most jobs. For example, a credit person must be able to receive phone calls and be near the files at the same time.

Annotated Bibliography

Books

Covey, Stephen R. 1989. *The 7 Habits of Highly Effective People: Powerful Lessons in Personal Change.* New York: Simon & Schuster.

The author introduces the reader to the important concepts of "paradigms," "paradigm shifts," and "principles" of behavior. Paradigms are maps of behavior. With the wrong map, we lose our way, regardless of our managerial intent. Covey argues that human effectiveness is based on a principle-centered paradigm. These principles transcend the values of individuals and organizations and frequently require a shifting of paradigms before effectiveness can be achieved, regardless of best intentions.

______. 1990/91. *Principle-Centered Leadership.* New York: Simon & Schuster.

The author continues his distinction between values and principles and the importance of developing a paradigm of individual/organizational behavior based on fundamental principles (e.g., trust). Unlike his first book, Covey goes into more detail on how to implement a principle-centered approach to leadership by looking at four levels: the personal (trustworthiness), the interpersonal (trust), the managerial (empowerment), and the organizational (alignment) levels. The book is a how-to approach to principle-centered leadership.

Both of Covey's books are important works for financial executives who are trying to get their arms around the "soft stuff" and trying to make it more practical for their organizations.

DePree, Max, 1989. *Leadership Is an Art.* New York: Dell Publishing.

DePree explains his views on leadership based on his experiences as CEO of Herman Miller. He explains that leadership is not a science or a discipline, but an art. As such, it must be felt, experienced, created. The signs of outstanding leadership appear among the followers. A true leader is a listener. Leaders owe a convenant to the organization, which is after all, a group of people. Covenants bind people together and enable them to meet their corporate needs by meeting the needs of one another. A covenantal relationship rests on shared commitment to ideas, issues, values, goals, and management processes. Covenantal relationships are open to influence. They enable corporations to be receptive to the person with unusual gifts or skills. The difference between a covenantal and contractual relationship has to do with intimacy, which is concerned with a person's relationship with his or her work, recognizing not only the skill but the art of a job, recognizing the importance of relationships, translating personal and corporate values into daily work practices. We must eliminate discontinuity between how we see ourselves as persons and how we see ourselves as workers. Relationships require honest and open communication. Everyone has a right to simplicity and clarity of communication. It is required to convey a common corporate vision.

_______. 1992. *Leadership Jazz.* New York: Doubleday.

Max DePree, Chairman and former CEO of Herman Miller, shares more of his personal views on leadership. Leadership can be compared to the performance of a jazz band, which depends on the selection of music and musicians, the environment, and the attitude of the audience. It exhibits the need for everyone to perform both as individuals and as group members, and the dependence of the leader on performance of the followers. A leader's voice is the expression of his or her beliefs. A leader's touch demonstrates competence and resolve. Leadership is a position of servanthood, and also a posture of debt and a forfeiture of rights. Leaders should treat people as volunteers. They don't have to work for the company. They follow only when the leaders deserve it. Followers can't afford leaders who make casual promises. Any follower has the right to ask many questions of a leader. For example: Will I reach my potential by working with you? Can I entrust my future to you? Have you prepared yourself for leadership? What do you believe? The very heart of leadership lies in the necessity of making it possible for followers to contribute. Followers need a chance to do their best. Leaders need a lot of help. The challenge for leaders is how and where to apply their beliefs to the daily stream of interactions with other people. A true leader cannot become committed without beliefs. In composing voice and touch, action must follow a sense of one's ethics.

Garfield, Charles. 1992. *Second to None: How Our Smartest Companies Put People First.* Homewood, Illinois: Business One Irwin.

The author discusses the weakness of values such as growth at any cost, the company as an independent entity, the company as a machine, and the pyramid organizational structure. He explains concepts such as the company as an ecosystem, part of a complex interconnected world, responsible to all stakeholders. The book provides current case studies on companies that are organizing by team, creating learning organizations, and treating employees as partners.

Kotter, John P., and James L. Heskett. 1992. *Corporate Culture and Performance.* New York: The Free Press.

The authors describe a study of the largest firms in 22 industries to determine the correlation between the strength of the corporate culture and long-term economic performance. Culture in an organization includes shared values and group behavior norms; shared values are less visible and harder to change, whereas group behavior norms are more visible and easier to change. Overall, there is a weak correlation between strength of corporate culture and long-term economic performance. Certain kinds of corporate culture help, whereas other kinds hurt long-term economic performance. Corporate cultures that encourage members of the organization to march in the same manner can help economic performance if the resulting actions fit an intelligent business strategy that is suited to the environment in which the firm operates. But even contextually and strategically appropriate cultures will not enhance long-term economic performance unless they contain norms and values that help firms adapt to a changing environment. The book cites numerous examples of adaptive and unadaptive cultures.

Levering, Robert. 1988. *A Great Place to Work: What Makes Some Employers So Good (And Most So Bad).* New York: Random House.

The author discusses qualities shared by companies that are considered fun, rewarding places to work. Such qualities include lack of social hierarchy, individual responsibility, opportunity for growth, opportunity to have an impact, continuous communication, trust, and employees' stake in success. The book provides details of 20 companies drawn from *The 100 Best Companies to Work for in America,* which Levering coauthored in 1982.

Senge, Peter M. 1990. *The Fifth Discipline.* New York: Doubleday.

MIT Professor Peter Senge's book introduces the concept of the learning organization. The ability to learn as an organization is a source of competitive advantage. Organizations, like people, may have learning disabilities. Senge describes five disciplines: personal mastery, mental models, shared vision, team learning, and systems thinking. Personal mastery is the discipline of continually clarifying and deepening our personal vision and seeing reality objectively. Mental models are deeply ingrained assumptions that influence how we see the world; we must be willing to reexamine and possibly change them. Shared visions inspire genuine commitment rather than compliance; people excel and learn because they want to, not because they are told to. Team learning allows individuals to grow more rapidly than they could on their own. It starts with dialogue, which, in contrast to discussion, requires people to suspend assumptions and think together. Team learning is vital because teams, not individuals, are the fundamental learning units in modern organizations. It is vital for the five disciplines to develop as an ensemble, and the fifth discipline, systems thinking, integrates all the other disciplines. At the heart of a learning organization is a shift of mind from seeing ourselves and our problems as separate to seeing them as part of a larger system. An important principle in systems thinking is leverage, where well-focused actions can lead to lasting improvement, but the opportunities for leverage are often not seen because people do not understand the structures underlying their actions. Systems thinking does not mean ignoring complexity. Rather it means organizing it to illuminate problems. Learning organizations move decisions down as far as possible. They encourage managers to take the time for reflection, conceptualizing and examining complex issues, rather than being excessively busy solving minor problems. Shared vision and openness to others' ideas can be antidotes to internal politics and game playing. Learning organizations address work-family conflicts by recognizing that such conflicts often undermine the success of organizations and that personal mastery and shared visions call upon an individual's entire range of experiences and perceptions. Senge cites Max DePree, who says that learning organizations enter into new covenants to support the full development of each employee in return for the individual's reciprocal commitment to the organization. In such an organization, leaders are designers, teachers, and stewards of a broader vision that gives the organization an overall purpose.

Articles

Barry, David. 1991. "Managing the Bossless Team: Lessons in Distributed Leadership." *Organizational Dynamics* 20(1):31–47.

Barry proposes that because many members of self-managed teams never receive training in group process skills, these groups frequently are unstable, tending toward fission rather than fusion. Leadership is a collection of roles and behaviors that can be split apart, shared, rotated, and used sequentially or concomitantly. It is assumed that each group member has certain leadership qualities that will be needed by the group at some point. As a result, a system of distributed leadership can be effective for a self-managed team. Four types of leadership that may be exhibited by different leaders within the group are envisioning, organizing, spanning (connecting the group's efforts with other activities inside and outside the company), and social leadership.

Brown, David E., and Edward E. Lawler III. 1992. "The Empowerment of Service Workers: What, Why, How and When." *Sloan Management Review* 33(3):31–39.

The authors compare the production line approach with the empowerment approach to managing workers in service industries. They define empowerment as sharing with frontline employees four organizational ingredients: (1) information about the organization's performance; (2) rewards based on the organization's performance; (3) knowledge that enables employees to understand and contribute to organizational performance; and (4) power to make decisions that influence organizational direction and performance. Manufacturing companies have made more progress in empowerment than service companies have. Federal Express is compared with UPS, and Disney is compared with Club Med.

Brown, John Seely. 1991. "Research that Reinvents the Corporation." *Harvard Business Review* 69(1):102–117.

A corporate vice president and director of a research center at Xerox argues that "the most important invention that will come out of the corporate research lab in the future will be the corporation itself."

The research department must design the organizational and technological architecture for continuous learning and innovation.

Drucker, Peter F. 1991. "The New Productivity Challenge." *Harvard Business Review* 69:69–77.

Drucker states that the single greatest challenge facing managers in developed countries is to raise the productivity of knowledge and service workers. He recommends that this be done by forming a partnership with the people who hold the jobs and entrust responsibility for productivity gains to these people. Continuous learning must accompany productivity gains. Knowledge and service workers learn most when they teach.

Engebretsen, Arden B. 1991. "How Key Is Finance to Corporate Strategy?" *Financial Executive* July–August:50–54.

The author, vice chairman and CFO of Hercules, Inc., believes that members of the finance function must have a broad knowledge of the company's businesses and the external environment and that the role of finance in supporting corporate strategy will be a factor in determining the success or failure of a corporation. He describes how Hercules adapted the finance function to a more decentralized team environment—for example, keeping the treasury function centralized but assigning senior financial managers to each business group. Engebretsen provides 12 truisms to guide finance professionals in their work.

Fitzgerald, Thomas H. 1988. "Can Change in Organizational Culture Really Be Managed?" *Organizational Dynamics* 17(2):4–15.

Consultants, researchers, academics, and journalists seem to agree that improvement in American competitiveness requires attention to organizational culture, which includes style, norms, core assumptions, decision procedures, and management attitudes. Consultants have tried to help corporate managements transform cultures by articulating new values and norms and using change levers such as role modeling, symbolic acts, creation of rituals, revamping of human resource management systems, and other management processes to support new cultural messages. Fitzgerald does not argue against efforts to change corporate cultures, but he says managements must first understand people's underlying values. He says that values, beliefs, and principles of the individuals in an organization are shaped by a multitude of personal, social, cultural, ethnic, and national factors.

Garvin, David A. 1993. "Building a Learning Organization." *Harvard Business Review* 71(4):78-91.

Harvard Business School Professor David Garvin acknowledges the contribution made by scholars such as Peter Senge in developing the concept of the learning organization, but contends that few managers really understand what a learning organization is or how to apply it to their organizations. Garvin defines a learning organization as an organization skilled at creating, acquiring, and transferring knowledge and at modifying its behavior to reflect new knowledge and insights. Learning organizations are not created overnight. Learning organizations are skilled at five main activities: systematic problem solving, experimentation with new approaches, learning from their own experience and past history, learning from the experiences and best practices of others, and transferring knowledge quickly and efficiently throughout the organization. Garvin says that whatever the source of outside ideas, learning will only occur in a receptive environment. Managers can't be defensive and must be open to criticism or bad news. Top management must free up employees' time for learning. Boundaries that inhibit the flow of information must be opened up.

Howard, Robert. 1990. "Values Make the Company: An Interview with Robert Haas." *Harvard Business Review* 68(5):133–144.

Robert Haas, chairman and CEO of Levi Strauss & Co., outlines the company's values and how these values shape the company's strategy and how the company is managed. Included in the article is a statement of values called an Aspirations Statement, one of the most comprehensive values statements the researchers have seen.

Konsynski, Benn R., and F. Warren McFarlan. 1990. "Information Partnerships—Shared Data, Shared Scale." *Harvard Business Review* 68(5):114–120.

Partnerships motivated by the sharing of information systems need not be based on ownership. Partnerships can create opportunities to cross sell and reach for a broader customer base. The authors describe four types of information partnerships: joint marketing partnerships (e.g., the IBM-Sears venture to market Prodigy); intraindustry partnerships (e.g., bank ATM networks and cooperatively developed industry standards for customer orders and status inquiries); customer-supplier partnerships (e.g., data networks set up by suppliers to serve customers, electronic data interchange relationships between trade partners); and information technology vendor-driven partnerships (e.g., various companies that have developed new services for their customers using such information networks as GEISCO and ADP). Managers should ask themselves what services can be offered independently and which can be leveraged through partnering. They should ask whether they can afford to offer joint purchasing incentives without confusing or eroding their existing customer bases. A successful partnership requires shared vision at the top, compatible skills in information technology, concrete plans to develop at least a few small success stories early in the process, persistence in developing and transmitting usable information between partners, coordination in procedural matters such as formats and codes, and a reasonable relationship between input and benefits for each partner.

Kotter, John P. 1990. "What Leaders Really Do." *Harvard Business Review* 68(3):103–111.

The author explains that management is about coping with complexity, particularly in the large organization that has emerged in this century. Leadership is about coping with change. Leadership has become more important in recent years because the business world has become more competitive and volatile. Articulating a vision and setting a direction of change is a vital function of leadership, one that requires a broad-based strategic thinker willing to take risks. Leadership aligns rather than organizes people and motivates rather than controls. Instilling a leadership culture in an organization is the ultimate challenge, according to Kotter, and one way to accomplish this is to create challenging opportunities for young employees.

MacDonald, Paul, and Jeffrey Gandz. 1992. "Getting Value from Shared Values." *Organizational Dynamics* 20(3):64–77.

The authors discuss the increasing importance of shared values, particularly in intangible information work, which requires implicit rather than explicit control. They provide a catalog of 24 values; different values apply to consensual, developmental, hierarchical, and rational cultures. Organizations may "make" values by hiring and training bright young people or may "buy" values by hiring experienced people who have developed values compatible with the organization. Changing values in an organization, which is not easy, requires getting people's attention (often done through a crisis) and maintaining the effort over several years. Integrating vision and values requires a disciplined look at the "hard" goals and the "soft" values and analysis of how they will mesh in the organization. Management must ensure that its shared value set is appropriate for the people who make up the organization, given their skills, goals, tasks, and cultural/ethical beliefs.

Marion, Larry. 1991. "The Corporate Ivy League." *CFO* 7(10):28–44.

The author presents results of a survey showing that Ford, GE, and PepsiCo are regarded as the three top training grounds for corporate financial executives. He describes how these three companies train their people and provides examples of people with extraordinary career paths.

Nonaka, Ikugiro. 1991. "The Knowledge Creating Company." *Harvard Business Review* 69(6):96–104.

The author points out that the company is not a machine but a living organism. Like an individual, it can have a collective sense of identity and shared purpose. This is the organizational equivalent of self-knowledge, a shared understanding of what the company stands for, where it is going, what kind of world it wants to live in, and how to make that world a reality. Making personal knowledge available to others is the central activity of the knowledge-creating company. Nonaka compares explicit knowledge, which is formal and systematic, with tacit knowledge, which is personal, difficult to formalize, and difficult to communicate to others.

Schonberger, Richard J. 1992. "Total Quality Management Cuts a Broad Swath—Through Manufacturing and Beyond." *Organizational Dynamics* 20(3):16–28.

Total quality management (TQM) is a concept widely discussed in manufacturing and service industries today. It overlaps some of the five management principles that are the focus of our study and will most likely be cited by a number of the companies we interview. TQM is aimed at continuous, customer-centered improvement. It requires data collection and employs multifunctional teams, brainstorming, statistical process control, problem-solving charts, and broadly based recognition of staff members. TQM emphasizes quality more than productivity and financial results. The author discusses the importance of continuous training and development, cross training, and recognition and reward systems. He recommends nonmonetary incentives such as process ownership, self-management, career growth opportunities, access to information, and removal of status symbols for the select few. Schonberger describes the traditional functional organization as an obstacle to TQM and describes the benefits of product- and customer-driven work cells. Work cells assume total responsibility for a product, which may be a final product, a component to be delivered to an internal customer, or an internal service such as order entry. Work cells are havens for cross training and joint problem solving and pave the way for quick response, better costing, lower costs and prices, and continuous service to existing customers of high-demand products. Schonberger cites some flaws of cost accounting in traditional functional organizations. For example, products in high demand may bear more than their fair share of indirect costs, and the resulting profits numbers may act as a disincentive to continued production of what the customer wants most.

Stata, Ray. 1989. "Organizational Learning—The Key to Management Innovation." *Sloan Management Review* 30:63–74.

Stata describes the United States's competitiveness problem as a declining rate of innovation. He points out that Japan was the first nation to rise to industrial power based on management, not technical innovation. Stata postulates that the rate at which individuals and organizations learn may become the only sustainable competitive advantage, especially in knowledge-intensive industries. He offers a theory that quality improvement is determined by the rate of organizational learning and compares this with the Boston Consulting Group "experience curve" theory that learning is a function of cumulative production volume.

"Should You Worry About the Future of the Finance Profession?" 1991. *Financial Executive* September/October:26–39.

Eight financial executives are interviewed about the most important changes that have occurred in their finance functions, where they spend their time, and what they consider to be the most important qualities for tomorrow's financial executive. Among the important qualities mentioned are integrity, ethical behavior, sound professional training, negotiating and people skills, ability and willingness to think and listen to the ideas of others, ability to persuade one's peers and interact with customers and identify opportunities, good understanding of internal and external environments, training skills, and leadership.

About the Authors

Henry A. Davis is a consultant and writer in corporate finance and banking. Currently director and corporate secretary of the Madison Financial Group, he has been vice president of research and consulting at Ferguson & Co., director of research and treasurer for The Globecon Group, vice president at the Bank of Boston, and assistant vice president at Bankers Trust Company. Mr. Davis is coauthor of *Lender's Guide to the Knowledge Economy* (R.D. Crawford and H.A. Davis, 1993), editor of *Essentials of Cash Management,* 4th edition (Treasury Management Association, 1992), and author of *Financial Products for Medium-Sized Companies* (FERF, 1989), *Electronic Data Interchange and Corporate Trade Payments* (FERF, 1988), and *Cash Management and the Payments System: Ground Rules, Cost and Risks* (FERF, 1986).

Frederick C. Militello, Jr., an independent consultant to senior financial executives of major corporations and leading financial institutions, is also an adjunct professor of international business at the New York University Stern Graduate School of Business. Previously, he was a cofounder of The Globecon Group, Ltd.; a vice president of the Chase Manhattan Bank, N.A.; and a senior editor and consultant with Business International Corporation. Mr. Militello is the coauthor of a book, *International Financial Transactions: Current Market Innovations* (New York: Globecon Group, 1984), as well as a number of articles, including "Swap Financing: A New Approach to International Financial Transactions" and "FASB 52: Changes in Financial Management," both published in *Financial Executive.*

Acknowledgments

The researchers would like to thank Mr. Roland L. Laing, former president of the Financial Executives Research Foundation, whose interest and support were critical in making this project possible.